MW00993490

CELEBRATING

CAPE COD & THE ISLANDS

Traditions, Festivals, and Food

KATHRYN KLEEKAMP

Other Schiffer Books by Kathryn Kleekamp:
Cape Cod and the Islands: Where Beauty and History Meet, 978-0-7643-5305-5

Library of Congress Control Number: 2020943539

Type set in Trade Gothic

ISBN: 978-0-7643-6165-4
Printed in China

Published by Schiffer Publishing, Ltd.
4880 Lower Valley Road
Atglen, PA 19310
Phone: (610) 593-1777; Fax: (610) 593-2002
E-mail: Info@schifferbooks.com
Web: www.schifferbooks.com

To my husband, Charles, who is a constant source of encouragement and support.

ACKNOWLEDGMENTS

This book could not have been written without the contributions of many individuals. First, I want to thank my daughter Liz for helping me create a potential layout, which simplified the chore of organization and helped me proceed in a straightforward manner. My husband, Charles, was willing to read and reread my work and, along with encouragement, never failed to offer suggestions and helpful remarks. His support was invaluable. I depended on many people to ascertain the history of the festivals. Although I was a stranger, they gave me valuable time and explanations, and for this I am most grateful. Chief among these are Brian Ahearn, Mary-Jo Avellar, Susan Avellar, Kate Bavelock, Allyson Brainson, Jan Butler, Mal Condon, Peter Cook, Mark Crossland, Annie Dean, William DeSousa, Charlene Donaghy, Bob and Jodie Falkenberg, C. L. Fornari, Annika Herman, Grace Hull, Keon Jackson, Sarah Johnson, David Kaplan, Donna Kutil, Judy Laster, Les Lutz, Joe McParland, Dan Murphy, Marnely Murray, Wendy Northcross, Dan and Kathleen O'Shea, Richard Paradise, Crystal Popko, Angela Prout, Rosemary Rapp, Bob Sanborn, Judy Scanlon, Mary Anne Sinopoli, Sarah Smith, Julie Wake, and Connie Wells.

Photographs were essential to the creation of this book. In several instances I asked organizers of events for images I did not have. In every case, they shared enthusiastically, and their generosity was encouraging. I also solicited recipes for food connected to the events. Thank you to the chefs, bakers, artists, and restaurant owners who took time to write their recipes, sometimes adjusting quantities for the home cook. Their contributions are credited under the images, artwork, and recipes they shared.

INTRODUCTION

Ocean breezes, sandy beaches, and quaint seaside villages beckon millions of people to Cape Cod and its neighboring islands of Martha's Vineyard and Nantucket each year. Travel magazines pay homage to bountiful fishing, sailing, seafood, and everything else this area offers. This is a land of enchantment, to be sure, but to truly know it we need to explore beyond sand dunes and salty air. Although a relatively small geographical area, it has an extremely rich and diverse cultural heritage. The Wampanoag Native Americans taught early settlers lifesaving fishing and farming methods. Intrepid nineteenth-century Yankee sea captains sailed the world seeking leviathans, whose precious oil lit our lamps. When the whaling and fishing industry declined, painters, writers, and playwrights arrived, declaring Provincetown the "biggest art colony in the world," according to a 1926 *Boston Globe* article.

Intellectuals and scientists formed an internationally known center for maritime studies in Woods Hole that in time attracted more than fifty Nobel laureates. In the midst of all this were those who quietly tilled the soil and created a landscape of beauty and abundance to complement the splendor of the sea. Fortunately, we have dozens of exciting festivals that celebrate, commemorate, and invite all to appreciate our history of maritime and agricultural roots. In addition, in a world-class tourist destination, many of these events enhance leisure time, providing meaningful entertainment and a way for visitors to feel part of the community.

Photo by Daniel McKeon

I first thought of writing this book when I realized that many people, even those who live here, are simply not aware of many of these exciting and entertaining celebrations. Those who visit only for a week or two may not have experienced the beauty of our harvest events, maritime days, art, and world-class film festivals. Off-season Christmas strolls in every village provide a charming and nostalgic return to earlier times. All these activities celebrate a distinctive people and history that dates to the seventeenth century and the many ways the region has played a significant role in our country's development. At the century-old annual Mashpee Wampanoag Powwow, Native American tribe members invite visitors to learn about their customs and way of life. Provincetown's Portuguese Festival and Blessing of the Fleet honors the hardworking fishermen in a town that was once one of the busiest seaports on the Atlantic coast. The fifty-year-old Nantucket Daffodil Festival recognizes the legacy of those who transformed a dark, gray island into a vibrant showcase of spring blooms.

Having lived on Cape Cod for more than twenty-five years, I've compiled a firsthand look at more than three dozen festivals on the Cape as well as Martha's Vineyard and Nantucket. Of course, eating is an important part of any celebration. I've included recipes gathered from local chefs, caterers, and restaurants associated by theme or location with each festival. An ethnic dish such as Greek pastitsio is a fun way to explore a different culture. Portuguese kale soup can be a welcome change from food not ordinarily made at home. Even corn dogs and fried dough can evoke happy memories of family outings. I've included these and many other recipes to allow the home cook to duplicate the festival-related foods. My hope is to make readers aware of the precious traditions that have formed this unique place, and to invite them to seek out new experiences on their next Cape and Island visit. Photographs are by the author unless otherwise noted.

Contents

10 *Early-Season Festivals (Pre–July 4th)*

10 Nantucket Daffodil Festival

16 Nantucket Wine and Food Festival

22 Figawi Race Weekend

28 Cape Cod Maritime Days

32 Provincetown Portuguese Festival and Blessing of the Fleet

38 SandwichFest

44 *Midseason Festivals (Independence Day to Labor Day)*

44 Independence Day

48 Cahoon Museum Brush Off Art Auction and Festival

54 Mashpee Wampanoag Powwow

60 Cape Cod Hydrangea Festival

66 Grecian Festival at St. George Greek Orthodox Church

72 Barnstable County Fair

78 Woods Hole Film Festival

84 Art Foundation of Cape Cod's Pops by the Sea

90 Martha's Vineyard Grand Illumination

94 Martha's Vineyard Agricultural Fair

100 Falmouth Road Race

104 Provincetown Carnival

108 *Late-Season Festivals (Post–Labor Day)*

108 Martha's Vineyard International Film Festival

114 Eastham Windmill Weekend

118 Provincetown Tennessee Williams Theater Festival

122 Nantucket Cranberry Festival

126 Yarmouth Seaside Festival

130 Wellfleet OysterFest

134 Martha's Vineyard Food and Wine Festival

140 Eastham Turnip Festival

146 Christmas on Cape Cod and the Islands

152 *Other Festivals of Note*

Early-Season Festivals

(Pre–July 4th)

Daffy Greeters welcome Main Street festivalgoers.

When March comes around, almost everyone here has the same wish: "I can't wait for warm weather and spring." Although winters are generally mild, they still feel somewhat desolate, given the short days, absence of lush foliage, and "closed until spring" shop signs. By April, there is a noticeable change in energy. Blankets of daffodils pop up along roadsides, boatyards begin to buzz, and families start to plan their summer picnics. Following are some festivals that welcome the new season.

Nantucket Daffodil Festival

For many who live on Nantucket Island, the quiet of winter is a welcome time. Tourists have left, traffic slows, and dark skies invite evenings of candlelight and cozy fires. However, when the island is ready to wake up, an amazing transformation takes place. Warm ocean breezes, sunlit days, and a brilliant show of daffodils erupt in a massive, island-wide extravaganza of orange, yellow, and platinum.

Yellow blooms dominate the Antique Auto Parade.

The annual three-day Daffodil Festival on the last weekend in April celebrates this awakening. Lining up to welcome the new season, more than one hundred exquisitely restored autos, festooned in blankets of daffodils, take center stage on Main Street. For three hours, visitors can mingle, take photos, and chat with the car owners. At the front of the long line is the restored 1927 American LaFrance Quadruple Combination City Service Fire Truck that served the town until the 1950s. It's driven by Rob Ranney, whose dad, the late Flint Ranney, co-originated the antique car parade with the late Jean MacAusland in 1978. At noon these vintage beauties depart Main Street and head to the village of Siasconset ('Sconset) and the highly anticipated mile-long tailgate party.

The festival is filled with many other colorful events. Youngsters parade their decorated, pint-sized bikes, scooters, and wagons at Children's Beach Bandstand. The Hat Pageant brings out extravagant, flower-laden chapeaus. Even canines have a chance to participate in the Daffy Dog Parade. There are museum events, themed walks, talks, and wine tastings.

The showcase event is the Annual Community Daffodil Flower Show. In the 1970s, Nantucket summer resident Jean MacAusland, a publisher of *Gourmet* magazine, donated a million daffodil bulbs to be planted along Milestone Road from Monomoy to Sconset.

Daffodils decorate Main Street's iconic lamppost.

MacAusland's goal was to beautify the roads for bikers and walkers to enjoy. She chose daffodils because they spread easily in the sandy soil and escape the culinary cravings of deer. In 1974, excited by her vision, fellow members of the Nantucket Garden Club organized the first annual daffodil show. Each year the Garden Club added bulbs, and soon hundreds of thousands of bulbs were planted in fields and roadsides with the help of volunteers and school children. Today more than four million daffodil bulbs bloom from mid-April to May.

Entering the greenhouse at Bartlett's Farm, the vista is breathtaking. We are told there are 13,000 distinct daffodil varieties, and it seems all are on display. Everyone, from pre-schoolers to senior citizens, is invited to enter their prize bloom, flower arrangement, artwork, or photograph. The exhibition is recognized by the American Daffodil Society as a bona fide daffodil show and grants ADS awards to specimens of merit. The Daffodil Festival serves as a beacon of seasonal renewal and hope. For more information: http://daffodilfestival.com.

American Daffodil Society winning entries in the Annual Community Daffodil Flower Show

All decked out for the Daffy Dog Parade

Dressed for the occasion, a visitor enjoys the Annual Community Daffodil Flower Show at Bartlett's Farm.

When those first warm days appear and spring fever takes hold, there is only one thing to do: prepare some delicious food, pack it up, and find a picnic or tailgate spot.

Farm-Grown Corn and Bacon Pasta Salad

Courtesy of Bartlett's Farm, Nantucket

1 pound pasta of choice
4 ounces smoked bacon, thinly sliced
1 tablespoon butter
½ cup minced shallots
4 cups fresh corn kernels
1 cup dry white wine
½ cup heavy cream
¼ cup chopped tarragon
grated Parmesan (optional)

In a large stockpot, boil water for pasta. Cook until pasta is al dente. Meanwhile, heat a large frying pan over medium-high heat and cook bacon until browned and crisp. Remove bacon from pan, reserving two tablespoons of bacon fat. Add butter to the bacon fat, add shallots, and sauté 4–5 minutes. Add corn, season lightly with salt and pepper, and sauté for 1–2 minutes. Add wine and cream and simmer for 5 minutes until slightly reduced, stirring frequently. Drain pasta and return to pan. Stir in corn mixture, bacon, and tarragon. Serve with Parmesan if desired. Serves 4.

Chicken Salad Sandwiches with Craisins and Walnuts

2 cups cooked chicken, chopped
½ cup chopped celery
¼ cup finely chopped sweet onion
½ cup chopped walnuts
½ cup dried craisins
½ cup mayonnaise (or adjust to taste)
8 slices whole grain bread
lettuce for serving
salt and pepper to taste

Place first six ingredients in a medium bowl. Mix until well combined. Place mixture and lettuce on bread to serve. Serves 4.

Chicken Salad Sandwich with Craisins and Walnuts

Nantucket Wine and Food Festival

Springtime ocean breezes, sand underfoot, chef-prepared food, and fine wines—what could be better? Over the course of five days in mid-May, enthusiasts from all over the country come to the Nantucket Wine and Food Festival. Islanders are friendly to begin with, but nothing says "Come to our party" better than offering 175 world-famous vintners, sommeliers, and award-winning chefs for nonstop tastings, lunches, elegant dinners, and educational seminars. The festival got its start twenty-five years ago as the Nantucket Wine Festival (sans the food component). As the story goes, in 1996 island resident Denis Toner and a small group of oenophiles enjoyed one day of wine tasting on the eastern end of the island at Siasconset beach. Over the years, with an assist from residents, local restaurants, and retailers, Toner transformed it into one of the most prestigious and anticipated events in its category. From that modest beginning, the event now draws more than 3,000 guests and luminaries from all over the world. Unique in its class, the festival is invitational-only, and the winemakers themselves must be present to pour the wines. In 2017, the festival changed its name to the Nantucket Wine and Food Festival, acknowledging the important role of the chefs and culinary events.

Left to right: Chefs Gerald Sombright, John Tesar, and Silvia Barban make final touches on food at the Continuum Dinner—Great Wines in Grand Houses. *Photo by Bill Hoenk. Photo courtesy of Ebony Hurwitz, CMP event producer*

Place setting for Great Wines in Grand Houses.
Photo courtesy of Ebony Hurwitz, CMP event producer

It's not unusual for more than 600 different wines from 150 prestigious wineries around the globe to be featured. Signature events are the Great Wines in Grand Houses gatherings. Ticket prices are not for the faint hearted—dinner tickets can top $1,000 a person. Nonetheless, tickets sell out faster than a rock concert! During these sessions, guests enjoy wines from world-renowned vintners and the culinary creations of visiting luminary chefs. All of this is enjoyed in the sumptuous surroundings of Nantucket's most exclusive private estates. For those who might like a peek into a grand home and not indulge in a full dinner, the Great Wines in Grand Houses Tastings event fits the bill.

Grand Wine Tasting. *Photo courtesy of Ebony Hurwitz, CMP event producer*

The events are seemingly endless. A recent event, Barbecue Redefined, featured a rustic, three-course BBQ repast, showing the differences in barbecue style from the Carolinas to Texas to Tennessee. Passport to Napa provided festivalgoers with a journey to the West Coast and the epicenter of American wine making, which boasts over 4,000 wineries. The Culinary Tent was an oasis of celebrity chef cooking demonstrations, food samples, libations, and entertainment. The culminating event is La Fête. During this multicourse dinner, attendees are invited to bring—and talk about—a prized bottle of their own fine wine to augment the selections being served. The historical roots for La Fête date back centuries, when vignerons celebrated the end of the growing season with harvest crew, family, and friends.

While the festival is all about fine wine and food, it's more than just providing a good time. Over the past quarter century, the Nantucket Wine and Food Festival Charitable Foundation has donated more than $1 million to local charities and nonprofits. For more information: www.nantucketwine festival.com.

One of the dining rooms for Great Wines in Grand Houses. *Photo courtesy of Ebony Hurwitz, CMP event producer*

A sampling of wines. *Photo courtesy of Ebony Hurwitz, CMP event producer*

Òran Mór Roasted Oysters Bourguignon. *Photo courtesy of Chef Edwin M. Claflin*

Edwin Claflin, chef/owner of the popular Òran Mór Bistro in Nantucket, is well known for his exquisitely refined yet casual culinary style. His creation below was served at the 2019 Nantucket Wine and Food Festival.

Roasted Oysters Bourguignon

3 dozen oysters
2 tablespoons extra-virgin olive oil
1 ⅓ tablespoon garlic, chopped
Fine sea salt
black pepper
½ cup white wine
5 tablespoons brandy
½ cup blanched, chopped parsley
1 tablespoon lovage, chopped
3 sticks Plugra unsalted butter, softened

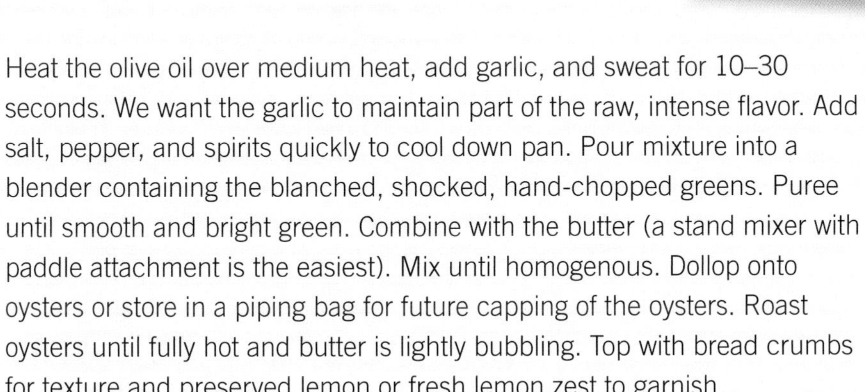

Heat the olive oil over medium heat, add garlic, and sweat for 10–30 seconds. We want the garlic to maintain part of the raw, intense flavor. Add salt, pepper, and spirits quickly to cool down pan. Pour mixture into a blender containing the blanched, shocked, hand-chopped greens. Puree until smooth and bright green. Combine with the butter (a stand mixer with paddle attachment is the easiest). Mix until homogenous. Dollop onto oysters or store in a piping bag for future capping of the oysters. Roast oysters until fully hot and butter is lightly bubbling. Top with bread crumbs for texture and preserved lemon or fresh lemon zest to garnish.

Note: Leftover compound butter freezes well for future use.

Figawi Race Weekend

Every Memorial Day weekend for almost fifty years, Nantucket Sound has been one of the busiest yachting thoroughfares in the nation as sailors from all over the Northeast gather for the eagerly awaited Figawi Hyannis to Nantucket Race. Although the 24-mile race is competitive, the emphasis has always been on the camaraderie surrounding the event. The race is a "pursuit regatta," with the slowest-rated boats starting first, and the sleek racers last. Using the PHRF (Performance Handicap Racing Fleet system), starting times are staggered between 10 a.m. and 12 noon. The idea is to overtake the boats in front of you, stay in front

Race Weekend flags catch the wind atop a mast.

Skipper Carl A. Merz and crew prepare *C'est Bon* for the race.

Skippers jockey for boats in the start area.

Crew members weigh down the windward rail to keep an even keel.

of those behind, and have all boats end around the same time of day. Scoring is based by order of boats crossing the finish line. The race annually gets over 240 boats and 3,000 participants. Racers compete in thirteen classes of boats, which can vary from a 24-foot J24 one-design keelboat to a sleek 67-foot Black Pepper Code 2. Boat names may suggest anything from shady movie characters (*Artful Dodger*, *Big Fish*) to Greek goddesses (*Valkyrie*, *Cassiopeia*). Various 12-meter America's Cup boats are frequently chartered to race as well. Former skipper Joe McParland, who has sailed these elegant thoroughbreds half a dozen times, shared his surprise the first time he got on one. "It was striking; there was nothing below but the ribs of the ship," he says. "They are entirely stripped out for racing, but boy, they sail like a knife through water!"

Boats typically sail a zigzag course to Nantucket. Racers in each class get their course assignment the morning of the race. Spring weather conditions, which can be unpredictable on Nantucket Sound, dictate. A recent Figawi race indicated eight different courses, each slightly modified for the various classes of boats. The race usually ends late afternoon, depending on wind conditions at the entrance to Nantucket Harbor. Boats then proceed as a parade into the Nantucket Boat Basin. Saturday night is a time to wind down and share the day's experiences while attending the Figawi Competitor Tent Party.

Spinnaker sails are set to catch the best wind.

A passing dark sky isn't unusual on Nantucket Sound.

Sunday is a lay day and a time to relax and enjoy strolling the island. The infamous morning joke-telling session, where no topic is sacred, starts the day. Around noon, organizers host a regatta called the Figawi High School Invitational, with fourteen teams representing area high schools and competing for the coveted Figawi Jr. Trophy. The young sailors, two per boat, race in double-handed, one-design sailing dinghies called 420s. After the town's Memorial Day parade, the day winds down about 5 p.m. Trophies are awarded to the top four finishers in each class, and other awards are given. In 1987, the Figawi Board of Governors added a charitable component. The Annual Figawi Charity Ball features a casino, raffle, and silent auction items donated by area artists and stores. It generates almost $200,000 each year and has raised well over $3 million for local charities. The ball is a fitting tribute to the slogan "Figawi: It's more than a race!" For more information: https://figawi.com/the-race.

WHAT DOES FIGAWI MEAN?

In 1972, on a foggy and chilly Memorial Day, Bob "Red" Luby and two Cape Cod brothers, Bob and Joe Horan, had a wager to settle whose boat was the fastest. They decided to race from Baxter's Boat House in Hyannis to Nantucket Harbor. The story is often told that at one point, in the midst of the fog, Joe Horan, coming up from below decks and realizing they were going around in circles, uttered, "Where the f*¢% are we?"—which, pronounced with the distinctive Cape Cod accent, is "fuh-KAH-we." When the race became official, Figawi stuck as a name that could be printed in the press. The sailors had fun and decided to repeat the event the next year, and the next. The race grew by leaps and bounds, and a tradition was born. Over the years, more than 5,000 sailboats have participated in the Friday-to-Monday weekend event.

After a day of boating, it's easy to work up an appetite for dinner.

Pan-Seared Parmesan Scallops

Classic New England Clam Chowder

Adapted from a recipe by Dan O'Shea, former commodore of the Allen Harbor Yacht Club, Harwich Port, Massachusetts

4 bacon strips, chopped
1 medium onion, diced
2 tablespoons flour
16 ounces clam broth
3 large red potatoes, cut into ½-inch dice
1 teaspoon fresh thyme, chopped
8 ounces cooked clams, chopped
2 tablespoons fresh parsley, chopped
1 cup half-and-half

Sauté bacon on medium heat until it's browned and fat is rendered. Using a slotted spoon, remove bacon to a paper towel. Discard all but 2 tablespoons bacon fat. Add diced onion to pot and sauté until translucent. Stir in flour and cook 1 minute, being careful not to brown. Whisk in clam broth. Add potatoes and thyme and simmer 10–15 minutes. Add clams. Stir in parsley, half-and-half, and reserved bacon; cook just long enough to heat clams through, about 3 minutes. Serves 4.

Pan-Seared Parmesan Scallops

This is the author's time-tested recipe for a quick and easy seafood dish.

16 large sea scallops (about 1½ pound)
½ cup grated Parmesan cheese
1 tablespoon flour
1 tablespoon olive or vegetable oil
1 tablespoon butter
Coarsely ground black pepper
Fresh chives or parsley, chopped

Pat scallops dry with paper towels. Mix cheese and flour in shallow dish. Coat scallops with cheese mixture. Discard any remaining cheese.

Heat oil and butter in 12-inch skillet (cast iron if you have one) over medium-high heat. When pan is hot, cook scallops for 2 minutes, turn them, and cook 2 more minutes or until golden brown outside and opaque inside. Sprinkle with herbs. Serves 4.

Cape Cod Maritime Days

Who isn't fascinated by tales of the sea, daring shipmasters, or the skilled men of the US Life-Saving Service who battled winter's raging surf to rescue shipwreck survivors. Some might prefer darker accounts of rumrunners and pirates, and they're here too. Cape Cod has thousands of stories to tell, and one of the best ways to explore them is during Cape Cod Maritime Days. This monthlong festival in May is approaching its thirtieth year and offers an extravaganza of nautical-themed activities that include lighthouse tours, museums, sea captain homes, boat excursions, and so much more. The nice thing is that you can experience them on your own time and at your own pace. Named one of the Top 100 Events in North America by the American Bus Association, the event offers four self-guided maps, "Maritime Meandering Tours of Cape Cod," covering every region of the Cape.

Whydah Pirate Museum, Yarmouth

Volunteer Keith Richards explains his model boat at the Cape Cod Maritime Museum, Hyannis.

The tour for Upper Cape Cod covers over a dozen sites, including Nobska Light, Woods Hole Oceanographic Visitor Center and Science Aquarium, and Cape Cod Canal Visitor Center. In the charming town of Onset, one can pick up a relaxing narrated ride along the entire length of the Cape Cod Canal.

The Mid Cape journey leads to Barnstable Harbor Eco Tours, Captain Bangs Hallet House, Whydah Pirate Museum, and Mad Jack's Percival's grave, as well as ten other sites on and off the beaten path. Of particular interest, the Cape Cod Maritime Museum on Hyannis Harbor is a gem of nautical treasures. Its beautiful fine-art gallery, restored maritime workshop, vintage craft collection, and Cook Boat Shop easily offer hours of insight.

Going a bit farther to Lower Cape Cod, you will discover boating excursions, historic Chatham Light, and a chance to get an up-close look at the restored Coast Guard lifeboat CG-36500. The intrepid crew of this legendary boat rescued thirty-two of thirty-three crewmen who were trapped when their tanker, SS *Pendleton*, broke in half during a violent winter storm off Chatham. Considered the most daring rescue in Coast Guard history, it was featured in the 2016 Disney movie *The Finest Hours*.

Coast Guard Lifeboat CG-36500 at her berth in Rock Harbor Orleans, Massachusetts *Photo by Marcia Bromley*

The Outer Cape Cod maritime journey invites visitors to fourteen sites along the coast, starting at the regal French Second Empire home of one of the area's most successful whaling captains, Edward Penniman. Going a bit farther, one reaches the stunning wilderness of the Cape Cod National Seashore and then continues on to the Pilgrim Monument. Most of these sites are free or have a nominal entry fee. For more information: www.capecodchamber.org/events/featured-events/cape-cod-maritime-days.

Old Harbor Life-Saving Station in Provincetown

Pirate Stew

Kids love everything about pirates. I developed this recipe for my grandsons. First, it makes beef stew sound more exciting, and second, it helps them understand what a ship's cook might have prepared on long voyages. With no refrigeration available, root vegetables were easily stored onboard as a staple.

Pirate Stew

2 tablespoons oil
1 pound beef, cubed
1 medium onion, chopped
2 cups broth or water
2 carrots, peeled and cubed
1 medium turnip, peeled and cubed
1 parsnip, peeled and cubed
1 sweet potato, peeled and cubed
1 tablespoon molasses
2 tablespoon rum (optional)
2 tablespoons flour, mixed in ¼ cup water.

Heat oil in a large stew pot. Add beef and onions and cook on medium heat until meat is browned. Add the broth or water. Cook on a low boil for 30 minutes. Add remaining ingredients up to and including the rum, and cook an additional 20 minutes. Add flour mixture and cook just until gravy thickens. Serves 4.

Provincetown Portuguese Festival and Blessing of the Fleet

Blessing of the Fleet parade proceeds along MacMillan Pier

To know the true meaning of the Provincetown Portuguese Festival and Blessing of the Fleet, it's important to understand the deep-seated traditions the Portuguese brought to this town. In the early nineteenth century, Yankee whaling captains, who sailed to the Azores off the coast of Portugal in search of sperm whales, recognized the skills of the hardworking Azorean fishermen. Their acumen as harpooners, honed over centuries, made them sought-after crew members. Azoreans, burdened with social and economic hardships, were just as eager to get away on the big whaling ships. In time, many of these Portuguese and Azorean men came to Provincetown and continued whaling and fishing. They brought relatives over, married, and created new families, becoming an integral part of the population. By the mid-1800s Provincetown was one of the prime commercial fishing centers and busiest seaports on the Atlantic coast. Booming with whalers, large Grand Bankers, trawlers, and open craft, it had a fleet of more than 700 vessels. "Upwards of 50 wharves, numerous packing houses, salt works, fish flakes, riggers' yards, and ship chandlers crowded the beach" (*OCEA News* III, no. 1 [Spring 1981]). In her book *Time and the Town*, Mary Heaton Vorse wrote that the Portuguese "brought with them their Latin gaiety and gusto for living." Today, 20 percent of the town identifies as Portuguese (*Cape Cod Times*, June 27, 2015).

Rancho Folclorico de Nossa Senhora de Fatima performers from Cumberland, Rhode Island, entertain with music and dance.

Children play an important part in the festival.

Fishermen carry the statue of St. Peter to MacMillan Wharf.

If you are fortunate enough to have fond memories of holidays at a loving grandmother's house with lots of relatives, family traditions, and more food than you could ever dream of, imagine it on a scale where the whole town is invited. The Blessing of the Fleet is always the last Sunday in June, and the festival opens on the Thursday before. The massive Seaman's Bank tent on the town green, under the towering, 252-foot Provincetown Monument, is the scene of most of the culinary tasting events. Situated next to the 9-by-16-foot bronze bas relief depicting the Pilgrims' signing of the Mayflower Compact, the huge canopy seats thousands of people over the festival weekend. Local restaurants put on "share our table" tastings and lobster bakes, but for most, the signature culinary event is the "all you can eat" Portuguese Soup Tasting. Waiting her turn to be served, Karen Walton from Chelmsford, Massachusetts, who's been coming to the festival for well over a decade, says, "I love this town, the heritage, and what the festival brings, especially the friendly, open feeling toward everyone." Beyond the great food, the more than thirty events include music, children's fishing contests, and a parade with costumed dancers. Most events are free. For more information: https://provincetownportuguesefestival.com.

The Blessing of the Fleet, which began here in 1948, dates back centuries to Mediterranean fishing communities. Portuguese families have always been keenly aware of their loved ones' difficult and dangerous life at sea. Sunday's activities begin with a Fisherman's Mass at St. Peter's Church to honor past and present fishermen. Afterward, a procession of local fishermen carry a statue of St. Peter to MacMillan Pier. Families and friends of the fishermen board their boats and

receive the blessing of a local priest or bishop for continued safe return and a bountiful catch. Don Murphy, director of the twenty-five-year-old festival, says, “Our organizing committee has over 800 years of knowledge of Portuguese culture, and everyone involved does it straight from the heart. We treasure our heritage, want to keep it alive, and share it with others.”

Portuguese fishing boats circle the harbor after the blessing.

TOP LEFT Portuguese kale soup is served from huge caldrons.

TOP RIGHT Mary-Jo Avellar serves John's Foot Long's version of Portuguese kale soup.

BOTTOM Hungry diners line up around the main food tent.

Mary-Jo Avellar is a lifelong resident of Provincetown. She has had an eclectic career, from writing, holding elected office, owning an inn, and, most recently, working as a real estate agent and part-time baker. The following recipes are from her book, *Provincetown Portuguese Cookbook*.

Jane's Kale Soup

1 pound kale
¼ pound salt pork
1 medium onion
1 pound linguiça
2 large Maine potatoes cut in large cubes
1 can dark-red kidney beans, drained
freshly ground black pepper to taste

Remove the stems from the kale and tear it into large pieces. Wash and drain. Put the kale, salt pork, onion, and pepper in a large kettle. Add enough water to almost cover the kale, and bring to a boil. Simmer 10 minutes, covered. Cut the linguiça into ½-inch slices. Place in a small pan and cover with water. Simmer 10 minutes. Drain. Add linguiça and potatoes to the kale. Simmer 10 minutes longer or until the potatoes are cooked. Add the kidney beans and cook until heated through. Serves 4 to 6.

Portuguese Sweet Bread

1½ cups sugar
½ cup butter
1 teaspoon salt
1 cup milk
5 eggs
5–6 cups flour
2 yeast cakes dissolved in ¼ cup warm water

Preheat oven to 350°F. Mix everything together. Shape into round loaves and put into large pie plates or round cake pans. Let rise. Bake 40–45 minutes. The bread is done when it sounds hollow when tapped on the bottom. Makes 2 loaves.

SandwichFest

Some years there's scorching heat, others the threat of rain, but visitors to the annual SandwichFest in the namesake town of Sandwich are never deterred. Held on the last Saturday in June, this rain-or-shine event is free and the crowds come early. The front lawn of the Hoxie House is the setting for massive food tents. The restored saltbox-style home, built in the mid-seventeenth century, sits atop a knoll and is believed to be the oldest house on Cape Cod. The quaint setting has a commanding view of historic Shawme Pond.

Inside the main tent, restaurant chefs prepare mountains of sandwich samples, hoping to win a People's Choice or Judges' Choice award. Recent winners have varied from a Cape Cod Reuben (lobster on grilled rye, Swiss cheese, homemade Russian dressing, and slaw), to a Fairway (sliced turkey, baby spinach, red onion, smoked bacon, brie, and fig puree on fresh ciabatta bread), to a more whimsical Elvis (peanut butter mousse and bacon ganache on banana bread). The nearby beer garden tent accommodates hundreds of diners who prefer a shady table. For a $20 ticket, hungry visitors get their choice of six different sandwiches. Eight to twelve restaurants usually compete. At 2 p.m., teams from participating restaurants circle around the judges' table, hoping to hear their creation crowned winner. Judges usually include the Sandwich police chief, a state representative, and the local newspaper food editor. Luckily for those who miss out on the tasting, the winners are required to keep the entries on their restaurant menu for one year.

The historic Hoxie House overlooks Shawme Pond in Sandwich. | Everyone gets a full plate at SandwichFest.

SandwichFest
Sandwich Chamber of Commerce

No one leaves SandwichFest hungry.

In addition to the food, Water Street, also known as Route 130, becomes pedestrian-only for the day, and almost one hundred juried artists, craftsmen, business members, and nonprofits line both sides of the street from Town Hall Square to the former Wing School. The festival takes serious note of youngsters, and canopies for nature exploration, craft tables, and face-painting are scattered among the tents. Hands down, one of the most popular events is the pet parade. It's mostly dogs that compete, but occasionally a pig or other four-legged creature shows up. While a DJ plays "Who Let the Dogs Out?," whimsically attired animals march along Route 130 to the judges' stand and vie for best costume and best kisser. For more information: www.sandwichchamber.com/sandwichfest.

Visitors enjoy canine tricks during the dog parade. | Visitors dine al fresco on the Hoxie House lawn.

SANDWICH AND SANDWICHES

The town name "Sandwich" comes from the Old English Sandwic, which literally means "sand village" or "place on the sand." The word for the food item "sandwich" is attributed to John Montagu, the fourth Earl of Sandwich (1718–1792). A profligate gambler, the story goes that during one intense session, he became hungry. He ordered his cook to prepare something he could eat with one hand so he wouldn't have to leave his seat at the gaming table. First associated with men's drinking parties, the concept grew as others began to order "the same as Sandwich," and Montague's creation took off. The modern "sandwich" didn't come into popular usage in America until Eliza Leslie introduced it in her 1837 cookbook *Miss Leslie's Directions for Cookery.* Today it's estimated that Americans eat more than 300 million sandwiches a day.

Lobster BLTs from the Sagamore Inn

Many of us have just a few favorite sandwiches in our repertory. One of the best things about SandwichFest is getting ideas for new and interesting combinations.

Lobster BLTs

Judges' Choice Award,
Courtesy of the Sagamore Inn, Sandwich

8 grilled focaccia rolls
1 cup guacamole
8 slices tomatoes
spring greens
8 strips bacon, cooked to desired crispness
¼ cup (or to taste) Hellman's chipotle mayonnaise
1½ pounds fresh lobster meat, cooked and cut in small pieces

To make guacamole, mash one avocado.
Add 1 teaspoon of the following: finely chopped red onion, lime juice, cilantro, jalapeno pepper.
Mix in ¼ teaspoon cumin. In a medium bowl, mix lobster with chipotle mayonnaise. Spread guacamole on rolls and assemble other ingredients on top.

ALOHA Sandwich

People's Choice Award,
Courtesy Holly Ridge Golf Club, Sandwich

8 brioche rolls
8 slices grilled ham topped with Swiss cheese
8 slices grilled pineapple
8 strips applewood-smoked bacon, cooked to desired crispness
honey mustard

Assemble ingredients on brioche roll.

Midseason Festivals

(Independence Day to Labor Day)

With the main tourist season upon us, sand, sun, and sea dominate the vacation to-do list. It's definitely a time to be outdoors. Plein air artists are painting seascapes and gardens, music fills the air, and farmers share their bounty on roadside stands. Ethnic groups celebrate their heritage and welcome all to their celebrations. Here are some of the fun events at this lively time of year.

Independence Day

July 4th on the Cape and Islands offers countless ways to celebrate our nation's birthday. It's beyond the scope of this book to list the host of events each town offers. There are parades (on water and land), concerts, cruises, fireworks, and activities galore. Following are some of the unique offerings. Details are available online.

Cape Cod

While there are fireworks displays in many Cape Cod towns, Falmouth's show has earned a reputation as one of the splashiest in the entire US. Some 50,000 people gather just off Falmouth Heights Beach to watch the half-hour extravaganza. Sandwich celebrates with more-modest fireworks over Shawme Pond in the heart of the town, preceded by an enchanting Venetian boat parade on the pond. Small boats with oars or trolling motors are decorated with Japanese lanterns illuminated by candles. Hyannis stages a pre-fireworks concert in Anselton Park and a boat parade in the harbor. Festively decorated floats, carts, tricycles, marching bands, clowns, and costumed dogs are just some of the sights one sees in parades from Bourne to Provincetown.

Lighthouse float in the July 4th Martha's Vineyard Parade.
Photo by Max Bossman

Nantucket

Thanks to the Nantucket Department of Culture and Tourism, Independence Day is filled with activities for all ages. Under the stately elm trees of Main Street and the patriotic bunting on storefronts, revelers enjoy trying their skill at a dunk tank and participate in blueberry pie- and watermelon-eating contests. At noon, the highly anticipated water fight between the Town of Nantucket Firefighters and the Boynton Lane Reserves cools everyone off. Sneakers are suggested, since cobblestones can get slippery. At 5 p.m., Children's Beach is the site of sack and wheelbarrow races, a tug-of-war, and other kid-friendly amusements. Live music on the town bandstand follows. The day is capped with fireworks on Jetties Beach.

Martha's Vineyard

Murdick's Run the Chop Challenge in Tisbury has been a tradition for twenty years. The 5-mile road race has raised over $100,000 for youth programs. Oak Bluffs celebrates the Fourth of July with a number of events, including the annual Kids Parade at the Tabernacle. Open to all ages, the parade begins at 10 a.m. and is followed by an ice cream social. Later in the day, celebrating one hundred years of community sings, the 2,000-seat Tabernacle welcomes all in a patriotic sing-along beginning at 8 p.m. The Edgartown Fourth of July parade begins its route at the intersection of West Tisbury Road and Pinehurst Road, and fireworks start at dusk. Some good places to see the show are Memorial Wharf, Fuller Street Beach, and the Edgartown Lighthouse. For more information:www.capecodchamber.org/articles/post/fourth-of-july-festivities-on-cape-cod.

Bubbles galore in the Sandwich Fourth of July parade

Youngsters have a blast with water guns on Nantucket's Main Street. *Photo by Jamie Holmes*

Who wants to cook on a hot July day? Even the kids can join the fun and celebrate making these easy, healthful, and in-season treats.

July 4th Berry Kabobs

1 pint large blueberries
1 pint strawberries
1 12-ounce bag white chocolate morsels
wooden appetizer skewers

Alternate the strawberries and blueberries on skewers. Place white chocolate morsels in the top pan of a double boiler over simmering hot water. Stir occasionally until melted. Using a tablespoon, drizzle the melted chocolate over the berry skewers.

July 4th Berry Kabobs

Cahoon Museum Brush Off Art Auction and Festival

It's the first Saturday in July, and you know something special is going on in Cotuit. People carrying lawn chairs and pushing baby strollers head toward the Cotuit Village Green, the center of this historic waterfront town. It's the annual Brush Off Art Auction and Festival, hosted by the Cahoon Museum of American Art. As museum director Sarah Johnson explains, "Featuring silent and live art auctions, artists painting on location, food, and live music, it allows us to connect with local artists, publicly celebrate their art, and bring the museum outside its walls into the heart of the community." She adds, "It's also our major fundraiser supporting all our exhibitions and programs."

As early as 7:00 a.m. artists begin setting up easels to paint *en plein aire*. The picturesque harbor, sailboats, homes, and nearby sandy coastline provide ample subjects. Around 10 a.m., visitors begin filling the large exhibition tents. Under the silent-auction canopy, festivalgoers crowd around paintings to make their bids, with the hope of filling that empty space over the mantel. For many, the allure of placing a winning bid is as exciting as bringing artwork home. Another tent displays more-elaborate paintings that are featured in the live auction. Johnson says, "The longevity and success of the Brush Off is founded on our artists. Most are strongly committed to the museum and have been participating for years, even decades."

Opposite: Auctioneer Charles Bailey-Gates conducts the Brush Off bidding.

At 1:00 p.m., the real fun begins when Cape-based auctioneer Charles Bailey-Gates commands the microphone. Part skilled communicator, part stand-up comedian, his charismatic personality instantly builds a rapport with the crowd. Expert at reading body language and expressions, he knows when to push for a higher bid or take a pause, always managing to get a laugh from the audience. Bailey-Gates, who's auctioneered the event for almost a decade, has as much fun as the audience. "I love art, and it's great fun helping to support the arts," he says. Those who don't go home with a painting still go home with a smile on their faces. For more information: https://cahoonmuseum.org.

A visitor and furry friend enjoy artwork under the silent auction tent.

Art collectors place a winning bid.

Cahoon Museum of American Art, Cotuit

Nuthatch, carved wood by master carver Erik Kaiser. *Photo courtesy of Erik Kaiser*

Summer in Cotuit, oil painting by Christy Peterson. *Photo courtesy of Christy Peterson*

HISTORY OF CAHOON MUSEUM OF AMERICAN ART

The Brush Off is the brainchild of Rosemary Rapp, who founded the Cahoon Museum of American Art in 1984. An art historian and collector of nineteenth-century paintings, she realized the need for an art museum not only to exhibit her collection, but to preserve the historical legacy of the home, studio, and work of Ralph and Martha Cahoon. Ralph was widely known for his mermaid paintings, and Martha for her charming country scenes. After Ralph passed away in 1982, Martha wanted smaller surroundings and put the house up for sale. Enter Rosemary Rapp, who says, "The moment I walked in, I knew my paintings would have a home." She bought the Georgian Colonial house and, in a gesture of generosity, permitted Martha Cahoon to continue living in a cozy apartment in the nonprofit museum, which she did until she passed away fifteen years later.

One of Cape Cod's premier museums, the newly expanded building, which blends old and new, can be considered a metaphor for the museum's wide-ranging exhibitions of American art from the 1800s through today.

Cotuit Oyster Co. Ropes Landing by Ralph Cahoon. *Photo courtesy of Cahoon Museum of American Art*

Striper, oil painting by Rosalie Nadeau

Many artists will tell you there is a strong connection between the visual and culinary arts. They share elements of form, texture, color, and, of course, creativity. Here are two favorite dishes from notable Brush Off artists.

Juicy Baked Fish

Courtesy of Rosalie Nadeau, Brush Off artist

oil or melted butter
2 pounds bass fillets (or cod, flounder, haddock, or halibut)
lemon juice
mayonnaise or sour cream
1 large onion, chopped or thinly sliced
2 thinly sliced lemons
smoked hot paprika or seasoned bread crumbs

Preheat oven to 350°F. Spread oil or melted butter on the bottom of a glass or ceramic baking dish. Rinse and pat fillets dry and place skin side down in dish. Sprinkle generously with lemon juice. Spread mayonnaise or sour cream liberally over fillets. Cover with onions and sprinkle with bread crumbs or smoked hot paprika, or both. Bake 15 to 20 minutes until flesh is opaque. Raise to top rack and broil briefly to golden brown. Serves 4–6. Note: The fish may also be grilled in extra-strength tin foil, tightly sealed.

Cape Cod Salad

Courtesy of Suzanne M. Packer, Brush Off artist

2 bunches broccoli
½ cup dried cranberries
½ cup whole walnuts

Wash broccoli, then trim leaves and some of the outer skin on stems. Slit stems in half and cut into small pieces. Cut flowers into bite-sized pieces.

Blanch broccoli for 2 minutes, rinse in cold water, and drain. Arrange cranberries and broccoli in deep salad bowl and toss with dressing. Chill 1–2 hours. Add walnuts just before serving. Serves 4.

Dressing

Shake the following ingredients well in a tightly closed jar, and adjust amounts to taste.
⅓ cup bottled lemon juice
⅔ cup first-pressed olive oil
2 tablespoons blackstrap molasses
1 tablespoon Dijon mustard

Mashpee Wampanoag Powwow

Now in its hundredth year, the Annual Mashpee Wampanoag Powwow features three days of authentic tribal ceremonies that are solemn, spiritual, and festive. The word "powwow" describes a cultural celebration where there is feasting, Native American drumming, and dancing by tribal members of all ages. While the Mashpee Wampanoags invite visitors from all walks of life to join their festivities each Fourth of July weekend, it is also a way to preserve important traditions. After years of holding the celebration on nontribal lands, the Mashpee event now takes place on dedicated reservation property.

Each year the Powwow has a theme, such as Honoring Our Traditions or Honoring our Spiritual Leaders and Future Generations. The day might start with "Mother Bear" gathering children for story time. Oral histories passed from elders to youth through song and storytelling are very important. Ceremonial dances such as the Eastern Men's Traditional War, Blanket Dance, and Jingles are vibrant and colorful favorites that excite the crowds. The daily Grand Entry procession with flag-bearing elders and other tribal members serves as the

Dean Stanton, visiting Narragansett tribe member, during the Intertribal Dance. *Photo by Elizabeth White*

"Golden Age" dancer wears a Native American Aztec costume.

Narragansett Native Americans perform in the Intertribal Dance. *Photo by Elizabeth White*

introduction to afternoon events. Visitors are asked to stand and men are asked to remove hats, and no photos are permitted, to preserve its sacred nature. Spiritual leaders are always recognized. Brian Weeden, chair of the tribe's powwow committee, says, "Our elders are the ones who've kept our traditions alive, and we want to honor them."

The sunset Fireball Ceremony is a highly anticipated event. In "The Origin of the Fireball Game," Ramona Peters explains: "The game came from an ancient medicine person who diagnosed the need for courageous energy, which the patient lacked." In what might loosely be compared to a soccer game with a flaming ball, the players dedicate their energy and courage to a loved one or someone in need of healing. The ball was originally made of deerskin and soaked in whale oil, but today's reenactment uses a ball made of cotton sheets, wrapped in chicken wire, and soaked in diesel fuel. The annual Wampanoag Powwow is a time for visitors to join Native Americans as they come together to celebrate their heritage, the wisdom of the elders, and their traditions. For more information: https://mashpeewampanoag-tribe-nsn.gov/powwow-info.

Young Wampanoag woman performs in the Blanket Dance.
Photo by Elizabeth White

WHO ARE THE WAMPANOAGS?

The Wampanoag Native Americans, known as People of the First Light, have lived on the Massachusetts mainland, Martha's Vineyard, and Nantucket for more than 11,000 years. A seasonal people, they lived near the coast in the summer to fish and plant crops. In the winter they would retreat to the forests and inlands to establish hunting camps. Once a robust nation of sixty-nine tribes, today only three tribes remain: the Mashpee, the Aquinnah (Gay Head, Martha's Vineyard), and Herring Pond (Plymouth).

Their culture is rich despite a history of being plagued by white domination, war, and disease. Wampanoags were a friendly people who helped the early settlers. The colonists had no working knowledge of the agrarian lifestyle they would have to adopt to survive. The Wampanoags taught the Pilgrims how to clear the land, farm crops, and fish the sea. In 2007, after a difficult process lasting more than three decades, the Mashpee Wampanoags were finally reacknowledged as a federally recognized tribe. In 2015 they were granted 150 acres of land in Mashpee, where they can exercise full tribal sovereignty rights. The Mashpee tribe has approximately 2,600 enrolled citizens.

Wampanoag Keon Jackson explains his necklace made of moose antler and tailbone. The tribe believes that killing a moose proves a man's pride and strength.

Food is a big part of the traditional powwow. Corn (also known as maize), squash, and beans were known as the "three sisters." They were planted together, the corn growing high, the beans twisting around the stalks, and the squash spreading out on the ground to protect the roots. Cranberries grew wild and abundant on Cape Cod and the Islands. Here are two Native American recipes using corn and cranberries, adapted for modern cooks.

Sweet Indian Corn Pudding

Adapted from a recipe by Plimoth Plantation, Plymouth, Massachusetts

6 cups water
¼ teaspoon salt
2 cups coarse grits
½ cup dried fruit and nuts of choice
1 cup milk
2 tablespoons sugar (or to taste)

Bring water to a boil in a large saucepan. Stir in salt and grits, stirring until the mixture returns to a boil. Turn the heat to low and cook gently for 10 minutes, stirring frequently. Be sure to stir across the bottom of the pot to keep the grits from sticking. Add dried fruit or nuts. Remove from the heat and allow to stand about a half hour or until the grits are tender. Stir in milk and sugar. Serves 6–8.

Cranberry Crisp

Inspired by Helen Manning, Wampanoag Elder

2 cups brown sugar, separated
¼ teaspoon cinnamon
4 cups whole cranberries
1 cup flour
1 cup oats
6 tablespoons butter, cut into small pieces

Preheat oven to 350°F. Mix 1 cup of brown sugar, cinnamon, and cranberries. Place in a well-greased, 8-inch-square baking dish. Top with a blend of the additional 1 cup brown sugar, flour, oats, and butter. Bake until top is brown and fruit bubbles, around 35 minutes. Serves 6–8.

Cape Cod Hydrangea Festival

C. L. Fornari gets ready for a session on hydrangeas.

The daffodil may be the official welcoming flower of spring on Cape Cod and the Islands, but no one disputes the fact that the hydrangea is queen of summer blooms. From July to September, the bounteous, globe-shaped beauties spill over picket fences, reign supreme in private gardens, and border waterfront estates from Woods Hole to Provincetown. Ranging from purple to blue to pink to white, they form bushes almost obscene in their numbers of blooms. For ten days over the second and third weekend in July, the Cape Cod Hydrangea Festival welcomes hydrangea lovers to events that showcase not only the flowers themselves, but all of Cape Cod. Local horticulturist, author, and lecturer C. L. Fornari, who jokingly says her initials stand for "compost lover," conceived the idea of the festival. She notes, "Although the festival is organized under the umbrella of our signature flower, the blue hydrangea, it's actually a celebration of all summer gardens in this region." Wendy Northcross, director of the Cape Cod Chamber of Commerce, enthusiastically agrees. "We love to look for ways to entice visitors to visit undiscovered routes on Cape Cod in order to appreciate the true beauty of our area," she says.

The many colors of hydrangeas

As Ms. Fornari was developing her festival plans, the Cape Cod Hydrangea Society was looking for a place to create a hydrangea display garden. The 100-acre Heritage Museums and Gardens in Sandwich stepped up and offered land for this use. According to Les Lutz, director of horticulture, the museum boasts the "biggest hydrangea display garden in the Northeast, with eight species of hydrangeas and more than 170 cultivars." Since the festival opened in 2015, enthusiasts have come from all over the US to see rare blooms, attend lectures, take guided walks, and participate in workshops, all providing ideas to take home.

During the festival, dozens of owner-maintained private gardens are open to the public. One recent tour included Marsh Mellow, a 1775 cottage featuring an authentic English country garden and more than fifty hydrangea plants. Calling All Kids from 2 to 92 featured a swimming pool surrounded by lush blooms and space for games. Flowering trees, arbors, and natural grasses beautifully framed a seaside home in another owner's Tranquility Garden. Plein air painters added to the allure of these beautiful settings. The Hydrangea Festival allows people to be inspired by beautiful gardens, learn new skills, and explore new places. Many Cape Cod nonprofits benefit directly from ticket sales. For more information: www.capecodchamber.org/hydrangea-fest-info.

The North American Hydrangea Test Garden at Heritage Museums and Gardens

HYDRANGEA MEANING AND SYMBOLISM

The hydrangea was first cultivated in Japan. The name comes from the Greek, with *hydros* meaning water and *angos* meaning vessel. Roughly translated to "water jug," it refers to the flower's need for lots of water and its cup-shaped petal arrangement. These bold and abundant, yet delicate, flowers symbolize boastfulness to some; others say they represent the heartfelt.

Artist Catherine S. Bergson paints in a sunny spot at Calling All Kids from 2 to 92.

Artist Rosalie Nadeau paints a scenic pastel at Marsh Mallow: A 1775 Cottage.

After visiting gardens in the Cape Cod Hydrangea Festival, one can participate in the hydrangea-themed Cocktail Trail. Covering an area from Sandwich to Provincetown, Cape Cod Beer and the Cape Cod Chamber of Commerce collaborate with more than thirty restaurants that create a special hydrangea-inspired drink. Here are some of their ideas for the home mixologist.

Flowers

Courtesy of Ocean House Restaurant, Dennis

1 egg white
2 ounces Glendalough Rose Gin
1 ounce hibiscus syrup
0.5 ounces Combier Pamplemousse Rose
1 ounce lemon juice

Combine egg white and other ingredients in a shaker without ice and give the mixture a long "dry shake" to create a velvety, foamy drink. After about 30 seconds of vigorous shaking, add the ice and shake a second round to dilute and chill. To avoid encountering any strands of escaped egg white when sipping your cocktail, sift the drink through a strainer as you pour from shaker to glass.

Hydrangea Buck

Courtesy of Cape Cod Beer, Hyannis

2 parts 888 Blueberry Vodka
1 part bourbon of choice
0.5 part lemon juice
0.5 part simple syrup
1 part cranberry juice

Mix all ingredients in a shaker, pour, and serve. Top with a Cape Cod summer!

The Hydrangea Buck by Cape Cod Beer, Hyannis. *Photo courtesy of Cape Cod Beer*

The Change Rose

Courtesy of Seafood Sam's Restaurant, Sandwich. Bar manager Riley Lewis tells us her two-toned cocktail is named after a little-known nickname for the hydrangea.

1 ounce Bombay Sapphire Gin
1 ounce hibiscus syrup*
Add Cape Cod Blond Beer to the top of a 12-ounce glass

*Brew 6 tea bags of strong hibiscus tea (available in most supermarkets). Add 1 cup sugar. Cook on low heat to reduce to a syrup.

Grecian Festival at St. George Greek Orthodox Church

Small Greek tapestries are for sale in the Greek boutique.

Does your dream vacation take place in a different culture, with warm and friendly people, festive music and dancing, and amazing food? You can travel to Greece if your wallet or time permits, but the next best thing is the Grecian Festival at St. George Greek Orthodox Church in Centerville. For almost four decades, this festival on the third weekend of July has attracted 8,000–10,000 visitors from all over the country. The culinary experience alone is worth a visit. Compared to other festivals, the volume of homemade food is on par with that of a cruise ship. Ovens and serving tables are laden with pans of pastitsio (pasta, ground lamb, grated cheese, and tomatoes topped with béchamel sauce), pork souvlaki, and fish plaki (a Greek-style fish dish baked in the oven with tomatoes, onions, and olive oil). The list goes on: dolmades (stuffed grape leaves), spanakopita (spinach pie), loukoumades, and more. The food is homemade by volunteers, and much of it is prepared on-site. You may not be able to pronounce the names, but you will experience culinary paradise. Michael Hayes, a Hyannis attorney, has been coming to the festival for twenty years. He says, "I enjoy everything about it. Tasting the food and getting a glimpse of the culture actually inspired me to take a trip to Greece."

Alex Herman and Ellen Efstathiou dance for onlookers.

Music and dancing make visitors feel like a guest at a large-scale wedding. Indeed, some of the dances are those performed at traditional Greek marriage ceremonies. The more melancholy Kalymnos Sponge Divers Dance salutes the sponge divers who came in from the sea with decompression sickness and could barely walk but still wanted to dance. If you have room after dinner, the kafenio, or coffee shop, offers authentic Greek coffee along with delicacies such as loukoumades, bite-sized doughnut puffs soaked in honey; baklava; and rizogalo (rice pudding) for those with a sweet tooth. One can even go all out with baklava cheesecake. Souvenir hunters can browse the huge indoor agora (market place) where Greek artisans sell art, clothing, jewelry, ceramics, and handbags. Local food purveyors offer olive oil and other traditional foods. Chris Kazarian, a St. George's parish council member, says, "We cherish our Greek heritage and customs and want to share it. Our whole parish is involved in this very volunteer-driven event." Opa! For more information: www.greekboston.com/event/festival-cape-cod.

Young Greek dancers find their spot in the circle.

Colorful Greek bowls on display

Pork souvlaki on the grill | Portokalopita (Greek Orange Cake) | Greek-Style Plaki

My family fell in love with pastitsio at the Grecian Festival. When I asked for the recipe, I was given one that called for 40 pounds of ground meat and would fill nine restaurant-sized pans! I've modified the ingredients to make a smaller and lighter version at home.

Pastitsio

1½ cups uncooked penne pasta
1 tablespoon butter, melted
¼ cup grated Parmesan cheese
Canola oil spray
¾ pound ground sirloin or lamb
1 medium onion, chopped
2 garlic cloves, minced
8 ounce jar tomato sauce
¼ teaspoon salt
1 tablespoon fresh parsley, minced
½ cup shredded Parmesan cheese, divided

Bechamel Sauce

2 tablespoons butter, cubed
¼ cup flour
salt and pepper to taste
1 cup 2% milk
1 large egg, beaten

Preheat oven to 350°F. Cook pasta according to package directions; drain. Toss with butter; add grated Parmesan cheese. Transfer to a greased, 9-inch-square baking dish. In a large skillet, cook beef, onion, and garlic over medium heat 8–10 minutes or until beef is no longer pink. Break beef into crumbles. Drain. Stir in tomato sauce, salt, and parsley. Heat through. Spoon over pasta. Sprinkle with ¼ cup shredded Parmesan cheese.

In a large saucepan, melt butter. Stir in flour, salt, and pepper until smooth; gradually add milk. Bring to a boil; cook and stir 1–2 minutes or until thickened. In a bowl, whisk a small amount of hot mixture into egg; return all to pan, whisking constantly. Bring to a gentle boil and cook for 2 minutes. Pour over meat mixture. Sprinkle with remaining Parmesan cheese.

Bake, covered, 20 minutes. Bake, uncovered, 25–30 minutes longer or until golden brown.

Serves 4.

Pastitsio

Barnstable County Fair

Late July may be hot and steamy on Cape Cod, but the 175-year-old Barnstable County Fair is up and running for one thrilling week. Thousands of beachgoers pack up early to get to the fairground gates by the 4 p.m. opening time. The midway games, 4-H demonstrations, live music, and food are just a few of the activities attracting visitors of all ages. Somehow "all ages" translates into everyone becoming a kid again and daring to try exciting rides such as the Zipper, Tilt-a-Whirl, and Scrambler. For adults looking for bragging rights, there are competitions for canned and preserved goods, baked goods, flower arrangements, garden produce, quilts, and other handmade items. 4-H youth are awarded ribbons for livestock and agriculture and many other categories. Of course, food is a big feature. Whether you're into chocolate-covered Oreos or fried dough big enough to carpet your family room, this is a time to put dietary guidelines aside. Lavender cotton candy? Bring it on!

A sweet first-place win for honey. *Photo by Elizabeth White*

4-H members parading cows in the Open Cattle Show

Goats always welcome a handful of treats.

The soaring Ferris wheel provides a bird's-eye view. *Photo by Elizabeth White*

The first Barnstable County Agricultural Fair was held at the County Court House in Barnstable Village in October 1844. It was a rather modest trade show for local farmers, consisting primarily of a few livestock and handicraft exhibits. By the late 1800s and early 1900s, it had become the most popular annual event on Cape Cod. No fair in the state could match the number and size of the exhibits. The Cape Cod Baseball League finals and championship games were special attractions. Then quite dramatically, the story pales. History tells us that each fair in the years following 1920 was less colorful, and attendance fell. In 1931 the Barnstable County Agricultural Society declared that the eighty-seventh fair would be its last.

Teacup ride is a favorite.

Opposite: Candied apples are a traditional fair treat.

After decades of unsuccessful attempts to reinvigorate the fair, organizers were able to purchase the Chesterbrook School in East Falmouth in 1973 as a permanent site. Since then, the property and fair have grown, with the addition of display halls, animal barns, maintenance buildings, and parking. The fair's success has enabled the Barnstable County Agricultural Society to give scholarships to qualifying seniors and college students on Cape Cod pursuing careers in agriculture, aquaculture, veterinary practice, or similar fields. For more information: https://capecodfairgrounds.com/events/barnstable-county-fair.

Herman's Hermits perform on the Main Stage.

For many people, fair food is just as important as the Ferris wheel or ring toss. When the season is over and you have a yearning for a special treat, here are a couple of favorites to try at home.

Country Fair Fried Dough (Elephant Ears)

Courtesy of King Arthur Flour

2 cups King Arthur Unbleached All-Purpose Flour
2 teaspoons baking powder
¾ teaspoon salt
2 tablespoons cold unsalted butter, cut in ½-inch cubes
¾ cup lukewarm water

Mix the flour, baking powder, and salt. Work in the cold butter, using a pastry blender, your fingers, or a mixer. Stir in the warm water gradually until you have a soft dough. Cover and let rest for 15 minutes. Divide the dough into eight pieces. Working with one ⅛ piece at a time, roll into a thin, 5-inch round, about ⅜ inch thick. Heat about ⅜-inch-deep vegetable oil to 375°F in an electric frying pan, or in a pan over a burner. Carefully lower one dough disk into the pan. Let it cook for 60 seconds. It will puff up on top and become light brown on the bottom. Flip it over and cook until light brown on the other side, about 60 seconds. Remove from the oil and set on a paper towel–lined baking sheet. Place in a 200°F oven to keep warm while you make the remaining fried dough. Serve warm with maple syrup, confectioners' sugar, or cinnamon sugar.

Corn Dogs

Corn Dogs

1 cup cornmeal
1 cup flour
¼ teaspoon salt
4 teaspoons baking powder
¼ cup sugar
1 egg
1 cup milk
3 cups vegetable oil
1 package beef frankfurters
8 wooden skewers

In a medium bowl, sift cornmeal, flour, salt, and baking powder. Stir in sugar, egg, and milk. Insert wooden skewers into frankfurters. Put batter into a tall glass for easy dipping. Dip frankfurters in batter until well coated. Preheat oil over medium heat in a deep fry pan to about 325°F. Fry 2 or 3 corn dogs at a time until lightly browned, about 3 minutes. Drain on paper towels.

Woods Hole Film Festival

Surrounded by the sparkling waters of Buzzards Bay and Vineyard Sound, the Woods Hole Film Festival (WHFF) is a life raft in a sea of mindless offerings at the local cineplex. The focus of the thirty-year-old festival remains consistent: showcasing the best independent films from emerging filmmakers. Over the course of eight days, beginning on the last Saturday in July and continuing through the first Saturday in August, filmmakers and patrons from around the world come to this maritime village to see great films, meet fascinating filmmakers, and enjoy the beauty of Cape Cod.

Settled more than 300 years ago as a quiet farming and fishing community, Woods Hole may appear to be a quaint New England village, but it's the epicenter for marine, biomedical, and environmental research. More than fifty Nobel Laureates have passed over the Water Street drawbridge to enter this world of scientific research, home of the Marine Biological Laboratory (MBL) and the Woods Hole Oceanographic Institution (WHOI). Breakthrough discoveries happen on a regular basis in this rarified atmosphere, so it's not unusual for the festival to attract a strong lineup of films about science.

Line waiting to get into screening of *Human Nature*. *Photo courtesy of Judy Laster*

Screening lineup for the 2019 Woods Hole Film Festival

oods Hole
m Festival

ID OR NOT TO KID
CLEVELAND INTERNATIONAL FILM FESTIVAL
OFFICIAL SELECTION
Sheffield Doc/Fest
2018
OFFICIAL SELECTION
DOC NYC
2018
tokidornottokid.com

Woods Hole
Film Festival
DANNY PUDI
EMILY C. CHANG
MAIARA WALSH
BRIAN THOMAS SMITH
EDDIE ALFANO
MARK FEUERSTEIN
BABYSPLITTERS
THE STORY OF TWO COUPLES HALVING A BABY.

Woods Hole
Film Festival

THE LAST
AMERICAN
COLONY
One Man's Revolution

Woods Hole
Film Festival

THE
WEIGHT
OF WATER
DOCLANDS
DENVER
FILM FESTIVAL
ashland
AUDIENCE CHOICE AWARD
BEST
2018
GRAND PRIZE
BANFF
2019

Woods Hol
Film Festiv
you gave
me a song
The Life and Music of Alice Gerrard

A FILM BY AARON HALL
MICHAEL LAKE
OVER
THE
LINE

THIS CHANGES EVERY THING
HUMAN NATURE
JIM ALLISON:
BREAKTHROUGH

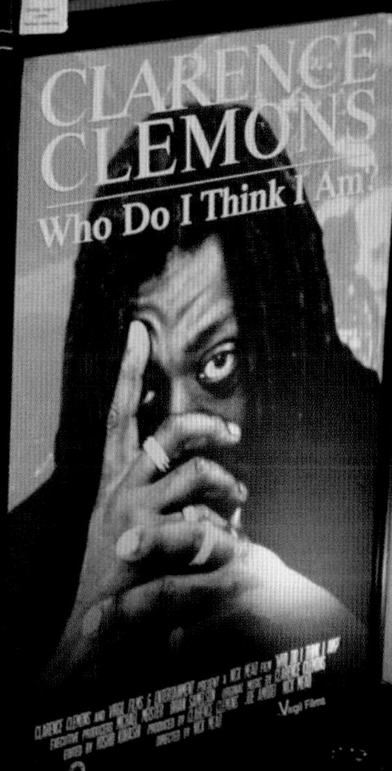
CLARENCE
CLEMONS
Who Do I Think I Am?

KATIE
SAVOY
WOLE
PARKS
WEDNESDAY JULY 31 8 P.M. OLD WOODS HOLE FIRE STATION
VIRTUALLY

Indeed, one of the primary goals of the festival, according to executive director Judy Laster, is to strengthen a long-term collaboration between film and science and to keep science at the forefront of visual creativity. Introducing the feature-length documentary *Human Nature*, about human genome editing in 2019, she told the audience, "My dad had a laboratory at Woods Hole. I've grown up seeing the power of ideas and the amazing way they connect scientific thought and the community."

Beyond films with a scientific bent, the WHFF also features an immense array of other genres, tallying over fifty feature-length films and more than 110 shorts. Intimate screenings take place in hometown venues ranging from the MBL's Lillie Auditorium to the community

Patrons wait for a screening of *Human Nature* inside the Lillie Auditorium.

Gutterbug film postscreening Q&A.
Photo courtesy of Judy Laster

center. Recent documentary and narrative feature films included works from Canada, Croatia, United Kingdom, and New Zealand. The four categories of shorts were dramatic, documentary, comedy, and animated. Titles ranged from *Where Dreams Rest* to *You Drive Me Crazy* to *Alaska to Hawaii: An Epic Journey*.

Panel discussions, workshops, and master classes focus on the creative aspects of filmmaking. A session on the challenges associated with making a documentary film touched on developing and pitching one's project, assembling a team, budgeting, working with the subjects, editing, postproduction, and distribution. Other discussions featured insights into the world of visual and special effects and how to extend a film's life and impact. This festival provides a chance to experience fascinating stories on screen and mingle with other film lovers and filmmakers. For more information: www.woodsholefilmfestival.org.

2019's filmmakers take a break for lunch by the water.
Photo courtesy of Judy Laster

Bourbon Caramel Popcorn

Whether at home or in a theater, no movie experience is complete without popcorn. The following recipes have an adult twist for the home cook.

Bourbon Caramel Popcorn

Adapted from recipesworthrepeating.com/bourbon-caramel-popcorn

1 4.4-ounce bag microwave popcorn (6 cups)
6 tablespoons unsalted butter
⅓ cup dark brown sugar
3 tablespoons light corn syrup
¼ cup bourbon
parchment paper

Pour popped corn into a large mixing bowl. Set aside. Preheat oven to 300°F. Line a large cookie sheet with parchment paper. In a medium saucepan, combine butter, brown sugar, and corn syrup. Over medium heat, melt the ingredients until they come to a rolling boil, stirring constantly. Boil for 3–5 minutes and continue stirring as mixture starts to thicken. Remove saucepan from heat and slowly stir in the bourbon. Once the caramel sauce is well mixed, pour it into the bowl of popcorn and coat thoroughly. Transfer the popcorn to the baking sheet and spread evenly over pan. Bake 20 minutes, stirring once halfway through. Let it cool 15 minutes before serving.

Spicy Popcorn

1 teaspoon chili powder
½ teaspoon ground cumin
¼ teaspoon smoked paprika
1 teaspoon sea salt
½ teaspoon garlic salt (optional)
3 tablespoons canola oil
½ cup popcorn kernels

Add all spices to a small bowl and mix well. Set aside. Put the oil into a large pot with a lid over high heat. Add the popcorn, quickly put on the lid, and shake to coat the popcorn. Let the popcorn pop, shaking the pan every now and then to keep the kernels moving. After a couple of minutes when the popping slows, take it off the heat. Add the spices, mix well, and pour into bowls. Makes about 6 cups.

Art Foundation of Cape Cod's Pops by the Sea

For thirty-five years, people from all over the world have enjoyed the world-class Boston Pops Esplanade Orchestra on the Hyannis Village Green for the Art Foundation of Cape Cod's Pops by the Sea concert. Keith Lockhart, who has been conductor for twenty-five of those years, says, "This is a fantastic place to be with a great orchestra, and a great chance to make music for everyone." Cape retiree Tom Osborn has been coming to the concert almost since its inception. "My young friends all wanted to go to beach parties and couldn't understand why I would go to a concert," he says. "I love all the Broadway show tunes and patriotic songs that are on the program. I've sat through the rain and was soaked at the end, but it was worth it to hear the music."

Around 5 p.m. on the second Sunday of August, anywhere from five to eight thousand (depending on the weather) music lovers begin arriving on the spacious lawns in the heart of town. There is seating for every budget, ranging from $25 to $5,000 for a VIP table. Attendees may camp on the lawns, relax on festival chairs, or enjoy VIP tables. As blankets are set and picnic baskets unloaded, opening acts by local musicians provide music from blues to rock, bluegrass, and more.

Opposite: Maestro Keith Lockhart welcomes the audience.

Stage and screen star Erich Bergen sings a medley of Burt Bacharach tunes.

The event features a famous guest conductor and guest performers. Past celebrity conductors have included Maya Angelou, Mike Wallace, Art Buchwald, Blythe Danner, and actor/singer Erich Bergen. Known for starring on Broadway in *Jersey Boys* and for his work on the hit TV show *Madam Secretary*, Bergen did double duty as both guest conductor and guest performer. After conducting a rousing edition of "There's No Business Like Show Business," he sang Burt Bacharach songs from Hollywood movie classics.

Each year there is an official Pops artist to capture the event. Past years have included Cynthia Packard, Sam Barber, Jackie Reeves, Jim Holland, and Cleber Stecei. The Arts Foundation is careful in its planning to reflect and celebrate an ever-changing demographic. Recently wine tasting stations and local food trucks were added. There have been more families picnicking on the Green and small businesses thank their employees with VIP tables. Family and friends can spend time together listening to one of the most celebrated orchestras in the country.

Ticket proceeds help its sponsor, the Arts Foundation of Cape Cod, fulfill its mission to "support, promote, and celebrate the arts and culture of Cape Cod in order to sustain a vibrant, diverse, and strong arts community." For more information: www.ArtsFoundation.org.

Orchestra members

Maestro Keith Lockhart conducts the Boston Pops Orchestra.

White's Catering in Orleans has been providing creative cuisine for weddings and special events for over two decades. Their food is a favorite of Pops by the Sea attendees. Here is a recipe for one of their popular items.

Seared Tuna on Cucumber Rounds with Soy & Wasabi Crema

Courtesy of Bob Oldsman and Chef Kevin

Tuna

1 pound ahi tuna (2 inch thick, cut into two brick-shaped rectangles)
Sesame seeds

Sear all four sides in hot pan, 30 seconds per side. Chill one hour. Roll in sesame seeds. Slice in ⅛-inch slices. Set aside.

Cucumbers

Stripe 2 cucumbers with vegetable peeler. Cut into ¼-inch slices and set aside.

Wasabi Crema

1 tablespoon dry wasabi powder
2 tablespoons water
1 tablespoon lime juice
3 ounces sour cream

Mix wasabi powder and water. Let stand 5 minutes. Add lime juice and sour cream.

Honey Soy Glaze

2 tablespoons soy sauce
2 tablespoons honey
1 tablespoon rice wine vinegar
1 teaspoon powdered ginger

Combine and set aside.

1 bunch scallions, cut on long bias, green part only
Pickled ginger, julienned

To assemble, stack in this order: cucumber, tuna, ginger, scallions, wasabi crema, honey soy glaze. Serves 4 as an appetizer.

Seared Tuna on Cucumber Rounds with Soy & Wasabi Crema

Martha's Vineyard Grand Illumination

First-time visitors to the enchanting campground in Oak Bluffs might feel they've walked into a life-size doll house village. More than 300 eighteenth-century gingerbread cottages in every delectable pastel shade offer a whimsical escape from the real world. When each house is adorned with glowing Japanese lanterns on Grand Illumination Night, the effect is mesmerizing. Thousands of people crowd the narrow streets on the third Wednesday night in August to experience this 150-year-old tradition. "It's almost over just as it's begun," says Lois Virtue, a resident of the island for more than fifty years and one of the last cottage owners to use candles in the lanterns on her front porch. "I like the soft glow candles give," she says. The campground's lanterns are set aglow for a brief two hours. Fire trucks keep a close watch, and Virtue has her hose handy.

Fragile Japanese lanterns are hung the day of Grand Illumination.

Colorful gingerbread cottages circle Trinity Park.

The Tabernacle dominates the center of Trinity Park.

Every porch glows from railing to rafter on Grand Illumination Night. *Photo by Michael Blanchard*

Religious camp meetings became popular after the Civil War. Oak Bluffs, already a vacation spot, was an attractive destination for a spiritual retreat. What began as a rather crude meeting place with a canvas tabernacle and tents for congregants transitioned into a place of permanent summer cottages surrounding a huge iron tabernacle seating 2,000 congregants. The Martha's Vineyard Camp Meeting Association became official in 1868. The next year a group called the Oak Bluffs Land and Wharf Company sponsored the first Grand Illumination Night, and it continues to this day.

The Grand Illumination Ceremony usually kicks off at 7:00 or 7:30 p.m. in the tabernacle. After welcoming remarks from the executive director of the Martha's Vineyard Camp Meeting Association, there is usually a rousing performance by the Vineyard Haven Band. The nation's third oldest, the band was founded in 1868 by a group of Union and Confederate veterans. Each year a person from the community is chosen to light the first lantern and carry it down the center aisle. Upon reaching the entrance, the honored guest hangs the glowing orb, which gives the signal for all others to light their lanterns amid thunderous applause. Although Grand Illumination Night is brief, the wondrous impression lasts a lifetime. For more information: www.mvcma.org/grand-illumination.html.

Linda Jean's restaurant on Circuit Avenue in Oak Bluffs is a short distance from the campground. This recipe, inspired by one of the restaurant's creations, is a refreshing side dish for a summer evening. Add grilled chicken or shrimp for a light main course.

Fresh Spinach Salad

1 6-ounce bag baby spinach
½ cup sliced strawberries
½ cup feta cheese
½ cup honey pecans
raspberry vinaigrette

Fresh Spinach Salad

Honey Pecans

½ cup plain pecan halves
1 tablespoon honey

Preheat oven to 350°F. Line a baking sheet or dish with parchment paper. In a small bowl, combine pecan pieces and honey and stir until pecans are evenly coated. Place on parchment. Bake for 10–12 minutes. Let cool for 10 minutes before using.

Raspberry Vinaigrette

1 cup raspberries (fresh or frozen)
¼ cup lemon juice
¼ cup white wine vinegar
¼ cup olive oil or walnut or avocado oil
3 tablespoons honey

Add all ingredients to a blender and process until smooth. Drizzle over salad.

Martha's Vineyard Agricultural Fair

Yes, there is a Ferris wheel, cotton candy, and baby sheep, but the Martha's Vineyard Agricultural Fair in West Tisbury is so much more than the typical summer festival. Brian Ahearn, president of the Martha's Vineyard Agricultural Society, says the "Ag Fair" is "part of island DNA." It was started 158 years ago to celebrate the season's bounty. Ahearn adds, "Farmers got together to exchange ideas and improve animal husbandry. Everyone involved had a common unspoken root." Jack Shea in "Simpler Times" similarly writes, "The Ag Fair, at its core, is an extension of everyday shared Island life." A visit to the fair, held in the third week of August, proves that indeed, it's a community-oriented celebration. The large exhibition space in the Main Hall of the Agricultural Society is literally filled to the rafters with handmade quilts, art work, and photography.

Opposite: Main display area in the Martha's Vineyard Agricultural Hall

Display cases and tables on the spacious main floor brim with prize-winning produce, imaginative flower arrangements, fresh-baked pies and breads, and gleaming jams and jellies. The Vineyard is known to have many fine artists, and this is evident in the handcrafted furniture. Even youngsters have their own display area for artwork, dioramas, seashells, and other collections. A fiber tent joined the fair twenty years ago as a way to teach sustainable practices and promote local farming. It's surrounded by alpacas, sheep, goats, and other animals that provide the fibers. Quilters stitch together colorful swatches of fabric, while weavers skillfully work the looms and other textile artists create shawls and sweaters.

Tradition is important in West Tisbury, the most rural area of the Vineyard. The fair museum offers an educational glimpse into an earlier time with its steam engines, antique tools, and other agrarian items. One of the challenges that Ahearn indicated is "How do we go into the future without forgetting the past?" This idea plays out in the food on offer. Alongside traditional deep-fried favorites are options such as gluten-free flatbread sandwiches, açaí bowls, and healthful smoothies. West Tisbury is a farmer's paradise, and the Agricultural Fair invites everyone to share the bounty! For more information: https://marthasvineyardagriculturalsociety.org/annual-fair.

Eggshells meet florals to win first prize.

Cabinets of baked goods are filled to the brim.

Young visitors get lots of up-close time with animals.

Summer Squash Casserole

These recipes have been adapted from *The Martha's Vineyard Cookbook* by Louise Tate King and Jean Stewart Wexler. They make good use of summer squash and tomatoes, garden vegetables that usually grow in abundance.

Summer Squash Casserole

4 small yellow summer squash, sliced
1 small onion, sliced
2½ tablespoons butter
salt and pepper to taste
2 eggs
½ cup light cream
½ cup grated cheese, cheddar or Gruyère
1 tablespoon freshly grated Parmesan cheese
1 teaspoon oregano

Preheat oven to 350°F. Sauté squash and onion in butter for about 5 minutes. Put in lightly greased casserole and add salt and pepper to taste. Beat eggs, then mix in cream. Pour mixture over squash. Sprinkle with cheeses and oregano. Bake until lightly browned and set, about 30 minutes. Makes 4 servings.

Summer Spaghetti Sauce

8 medium tomatoes, coarsely chopped
1 6-ounce can tomato paste
½ cup olive oil
6–8 large garlic cloves, minced
1 large green pepper, coarsely chopped
1 medium onion, coarsely chopped
1 cup chopped parsley, loosely packed
1 teaspoon salt
freshly grated Parmesan or Romano cheese

Combine all ingredients except cheese in a 3-quart kettle. Stir to mix. Bring to a boil over high heat, then lower heat and cook sauce slowly for at least 1 hour. Stir occasionally to prevent sticking. Serve hot over freshly cooked pasta; sprinkle with grated Parmesan or Romano cheese. Makes 6–8 servings.

Falmouth Road Race

It all began when Tommy Leonard, a bartender and running enthusiast, worked at the Brothers Four club in Falmouth. He was watching the 1972 Munich Olympics and was awed by a runner named Frank Shorter. The story goes that he became so engrossed in the race and the young man's win (first American since 1908 to win the Olympic marathon) that he shut down the bar. History quotes Leonard as saying, "Wouldn't it be fantastic if we could get Frank Shorter to run in a race on Cape Cod?" Along with Falmouth track coach John Carroll and an assist by the town recreation director, Rich Sherman, he organized the first race in 1973 with ninety-three participants. In 1975 Tommy Leonard's dream came true. Olympic gold medalist Frank Shorter came to Falmouth and won the 1975 race, which had grown to more than 850 participants. Today, the New Balance Falmouth Road Race, held the third Sunday in August, is one of the premier running events of the summer season. From Shorter's early vision, it has swelled to more than 11,000 runners and attained world-class status for novice as well as elite athletes. Carroll and Sherman along with their wives, Lucia and Kathy, respectively, served as race directors for thirty-eight years until March 2011. There are three race divisions: Wheelchair, Elite Women, and Elite Men & Open.

Leonard Korir, the first American to win the Falmouth Road Race.
Photo courtesy of Falmouth Road Race, Inc.

Aerial view of runners passing Nobska Lighthouse.
Photo courtesy of Falmouth Road Race, Inc.

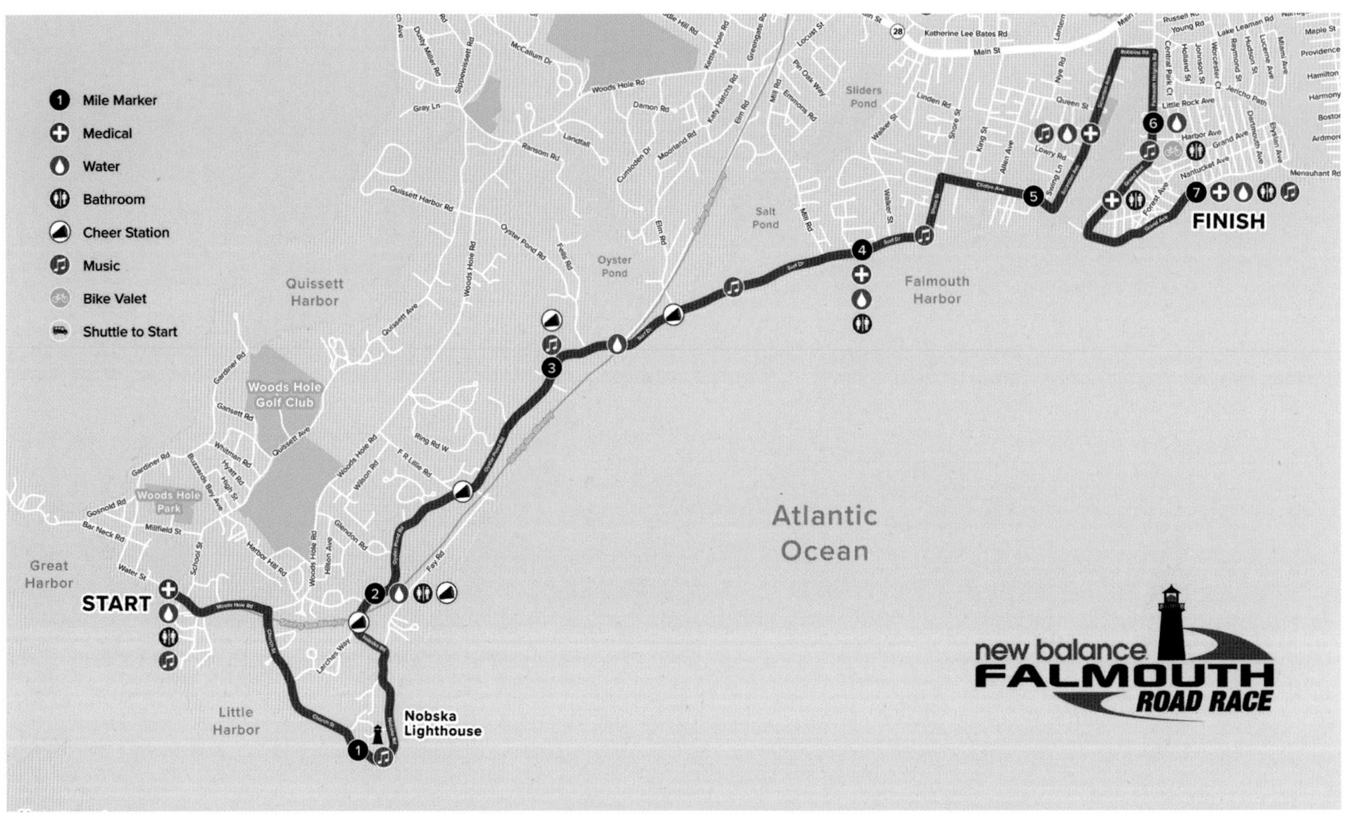

One of the most beautiful seaside courses to run, the 7-mile race begins in front of the community center in Woods Hole. Proceeding out of town, it winds around Nobska Lighthouse and continues along the hilly, tree-lined road, then opens up to 1.5 miles along the beach overlooking Vineyard Sound. Runners loop around Falmouth Inner Harbor, then go up a small, steep hill to Falmouth Heights and down to the finish line along Grand Avenue at Falmouth Heights Beach. The race also has a significant charitable outreach. In 2018 its charity teams raised a record $4.9 million. For more information: https://falmouthroadrace.com.

Falmouth Road Race Map.
Photo courtesy of Falmouth Road Race, Inc.

What is more refreshing than a smoothie? After a run or workout, when you're thirsty and need to replenish carbohydrates, these drinks tick all the boxes.

Blueberry Peach Smoothie

1 cup frozen blueberries
1 cup frozen peaches
1 cup Greek yogurt (any flavor you prefer)
A dozen raw almonds
½ cup almond milk or other nut milk of choice

Put all ingredients into a blender and mix until smooth, about 30 seconds.

Banana Peanut Butter Smoothie

2 bananas, broken into chunks
2 cups milk
¼ cup peanut butter
1–2 tablespoons honey
1 cup ice cubes

Put all ingredients in a blender and mix until smooth. For an extra treat, add 1 tablespoon of cocoa powder or 1–2 tablespoons chocolate syrup.

Banana Peanut Butter Smoothie

Provincetown Carnival

Cape Cod's weeklong "party to end all parties" has to be Provincetown's Carnival, which attracts more than 100,000 visitors. If, as we are told, Provincetown is a feast, then Carnival is a fantastical kingdom where glamour and fantasy rule. Hands down, the festival's crowning event is the Carnival Parade. Businesses, groups, and individuals create flamboyant floats around themes such as Gods and Goddesses, Mardi Gras by the Sea, and the Enchanted Forest.

This extravaganza is filled with marching groups, bands, bikes, pull carts, and grand marshals. Dazzling costumes and as much glitz as the body can hold are the order of the day.

The four-decade-old celebration had humble beginnings in the effort to bring attention to the brand-new Provincetown Business Guild (PBG). In 1978 a small number of local gay and straight business owners banded together to promote Provincetown as a vacation spot for gay and lesbian tourists. The third week in August was slow in tourist traffic, and organizers thought that a parade that culminated in a party would attract more people. Herbie Hintz, a longtime Provincetown resident who walked in that first parade, fondly recalls, "There were thirteen of us, and only three guesthouses had floats. No one even knew it was a parade!" The theme was A Night in Rio, and a tradition began. Annual themes are a mainstay of Carnival!

Carnival revelers on Commercial Street

Commercial Street is filled with music during Carnival.
Photo by Daniel McKeon

The week is also filled with cruises, pool parties, costume balls, drag shows, and cocktail receptions. Provincetown is considered America's oldest continuous art colony, and art galleries line Commercial Street from the east to west ends. On Friday evening, gallery owners offer open studios, viewings, and receptions for local artists. For those looking for a break from the heat and hoopla, ocean breezes and quiet beaches are a short walk away. For more information: www.ptown.org/provincetown-carnival.

Here comes the bride. *Photo by Daniel McKeon*

The Lobster Pot Restaurant is in the heart of Provincetown. Its iconic, bright-red neon lobster sign has been welcoming diners to enjoy its fresh seafood and harbor views for generations. Try the following dish on a late-summer day. Recipe courtesy of chef/owner Tim McNulty from his *Lobster Pot Cookbook.*

Lobster-Avocado Cocktail

5 ounces fresh-picked lobster meat, cut into bite-size pieces
1 avocado, diced
1 teaspoon each of red, yellow, orange, and green bell pepper, finely diced
juice of 1 orange
juice of 1 lime
juice of 1 lemon
1 tablespoon rice wine vinegar
coarse sea salt and coarse black pepper to taste
1 teaspoon sugar
1 tablespoon fresh cilantro, chopped (or to taste)
1 cup iceberg lettuce, shredded

The Lobster Pot Restaurant in Provincetown

Tarragon Mayonnaise

2 tablespoons mayonnaise
¼ teaspoon Dijon mustard
½ teaspoon shallots, finely diced
½ teaspoon fresh tarragon, chopped
juice of 1 lemon
pinch of black pepper

Prepare the mayonnaise. Place all ingredients in a bowl and mix together. Do this at least a couple of hours ahead so that ingredients will marry nicely. Then mix lobster-avocado ingredients in a bowl except for the iceberg. To serve, place the lobster-avocado mixture on top of the lettuce and add a dollop of mayonnaise. Makes 2 servings.

Late-Season Festivals

(Post–Labor Day)

The Martha's Vineyard Film Center shows art-house film programming and performances throughout the year. *Photo courtesy of Richard Paradise*

As days become shorter and kids go back to school, many people board up their summer homes and say a fond farewell to the beach. However, for others, this "shoulder season" is the best time to appreciate all the area has to offer. Many activities switch to indoors, and cultural events abound. Farmers and fishermen celebrate the season by inviting all to partake of their bounty. When the holidays arrive, every town celebrates in its own way. Here are some ways to join in.

Martha's Vineyard International Film Festival

In 1999 a small group of Island movie buffs got together on summer Thursday evenings to watch 16 mm classic and cult movies on wooden benches in the Grange Hall in West Tisbury. From that event, a small band of volunteers, led by founder Richard Paradise, formed the Martha's Vineyard Film Society. Now employing more than twenty people in summer, and with an annual operating budget of over $1 million, the group produced the first Martha's Vineyard International Film Festival (MVIFF) in 2006.

Richard Paradise, executive director of the MVIFF, chats with actress Sharon Stone, recipient of the Global Citizen Humanitarian Award. *Photo by Max Bossman*

Over six festival days in early September, hundreds of film lovers stream between the state-of-the-art Martha's Vineyard Film Center and the historic Capawock Theater on Main Street in Vineyard Haven. These theaters are filled with the best feature films and shorts drawn from every world region, including Latin America, the Middle and Far East, Africa, and the UK. With a recurring theme of Other Places, Other People, 90 percent of offerings are non-US productions to promote cross-cultural understanding. Entries come from festivals such as Sundance, Tokyo, and Berlin. Postfilm "conversations," whether in person or via Skype, allow directors, film writers, and others involved with the films to engage in lively discussions with audience members.

Features have included *Cold Case Hammarskjöld*, a documentary by Danish filmmaker Mads Brügger, which plays like a thriller and addresses the mysterious crash of the United Nations secretary general's airplane in 1961. *The Bra*, a tragicomedy by German director Veit Helmer, was unique in being totally without dialogue. The protagonist is a lonely, soon-to-retire train driver seeking to discover love by finding the owner of the bra his train snagged from a clothesline. Helmer was in attendance and shared his view that telling a story without words is the purest form of film art, since language separates us from other people and countries.

Audience members await a screening inside the Martha's Vineyard Film Center. *Photo courtesy of Richard Paradise*

Scene from director Veit Helmer's *The Bra*, starring Paz Vega. *Photo courtesy of Veit Helmer*

Ten short films were chosen as finalists from more than 350 entries, indicating the broad interest in the MVIFF. A special presentation in the 2019 festival was "Animated Shorts," curated by Oscar nominee Bill Plympton, one of several acclaimed filmmakers who attend the festival. *Moviemaker* magazine has recognized the MVIFF several times as one of the "50 Film Festivals Worth the Entry Fee." The Vineyard's laid-back ambience and its Walking Festival District, featuring shops, restaurants, special events, and live music, make the festival well worth the forty-five-minute ferry ride.

For more information: https://marthas-vineyard.com/events-calendar/Marthas-vineyard-international-film-festival.

Theatergoers wait in line to see a screening.
Photo courtesy of Richard Paradise

Here are two easy movie-themed recipes to try before going to the cinema or streaming a film at home.

Pasta Aglio e Olio

Inspired by a dish in the film *Chef*

1 pound dried spaghetti
½ cup extra virgin olive oil
6 garlic cloves, minced
1 teaspoon crushed red pepper flakes
½ cup fresh parsley, minced
¼ cup fresh basil, minced
½ cup Parmesan cheese
salt and pepper to taste

Bring a large pot of salted water to boil. Add the spaghetti and cook until al dente, 8–10 minutes. Drain. Heat olive oil in a large pan over medium heat. Add garlic, stirring frequently until golden in color. Add the drained spaghetti directly to the pan. Toss until spaghetti is thoroughly coated with the olive oil. Remove from heat. Add red pepper flakes, parsley, basil, Parmesan cheese, salt, and pepper, and toss well. Garnish with more Parmesan. Makes 4 servings.

Southern Fried Chicken

Inspired by one of the mouth-watering dishes in the movie *The Help*

4 skinless chicken legs
4 skinless chicken thighs
1 cup low-fat buttermilk
salt and pepper to taste
1½ cups flour
2 tablespoons sweet paprika
1 tablespoon finely chopped fresh rosemary leaves
1 cup vegetable oil

Preheat oven to 450°F. Line one large, rimmed baking sheet with aluminum foil. In a large bowl or pan, combine chicken, buttermilk, salt, and pepper. Set aside for 5–10 minutes. In another medium bowl, whisk together flour, paprika, rosemary, salt, and pepper. Dip each piece of chicken in buttermilk, allowing excess to drip off, and dredge in flour mixture. Shake off excess. Place on clean dish until ready to fry. In a 12-inch cast-iron skillet, heat oil over medium-high. Fry chicken until golden brown, 4–5 minutes per side. If chicken browns too quickly, reduce heat. Drain excess oil and transfer to baking pan lined with aluminum foil. Bake chicken until an instant-read thermometer inserted in thickest part of a thigh registers 165°F, 15–20 minutes. Let cool 5 minutes before serving. Serves 4.

Eastham Windmill Weekend

Windmills are an important part of Cape Cod's charm. Whether used for milling corn or pumping seawater to manufacture salt, they were critical to early settlers. The few that remain are beloved and serve as centerpieces of their communities. The Eastham windmill is believed to be the oldest on Cape Cod, dating to 1680. The town's scenic Windmill Village Green comes alive the first weekend after Labor Day, starting Friday night and running through Sunday, as the town holds its annual Windmill Weekend to honor its iconic landmark. This old-fashioned small-town event has celebrated life on the Outer Cape for over four decades. "I love knowing that individuals and families are having fun at an affordable price and we are raising funds to benefit local organizations," says festival director Sarah Smith, a lifelong resident. Clearly, the almost 2,000 annual visitors agree.

The event kicks off with a Friday evening chicken and fish fry at the Elks lodge, followed by a community talent show. Dancing plumbers, singing electricians—all are welcome to perform, with an assist from a professional sound system and keyboard. Saturday is filled with band concerts on the village green, museum events, family games, and an arts-and-crafts show with dozens of vendor tents. The Great Tricycle Race creates lots of laughs as adults and kids try to maneuver pint-sized trikes. The joke is that face painting is Massachusetts state law wherever there is a gathering with kids. You'll find it here, along with balloon animals and children's games; all are sponsored by local

Activities are planned with both adults and kids in mind. *Photo courtesy of Sarah Smith*

Volunteer Steve Garran puts on his wet suit each year to take hits in the dunk tank.

Windmill Park is filled with visitors on festival days.

organizations, making it easy on parents' pocketbooks. Weather permitting, a sand art contest is held on First Encounter Beach, named for the site where the Pilgrims had their first skirmish with Native Americans. Sunday morning starts with a 5K road race, followed by a half-mile children's fun run for kids under ten. The themed windmill parade, quaint with homemade floats, costumed dogs, youth groups, and local musicians, always gets enthusiastic shouts from appreciative onlookers. For more information: https://easthamwindmillweekend.org.

Cod Cakes with Aioli and Black Bean & Corn Salad

A twenty-year resident of Eastham, Mary P. Bakas has been cooking ever since she can remember. After traveling the world (on her bike, no less) and experiencing many cuisines, she settled down on Cape Cod to raise her family. After cooking for upper-tier caterers in Provincetown, she opened a commercial catering service in Chatham. The following recipe is courtesy of Mary P. Bakas, Mary's Fine Provisions.

Cod Cakes with Aioli

2 pounds fresh, skinless cod fish
4 tablespoons olive oil, divided
4 or 5 medium-sized red potatoes, unpeeled
1 medium onion, finely chopped
1 red bell pepper, finely chopped
2 celery ribs, finely chopped
olive oil
½ teaspoon dried chili flakes
salt and pepper to taste
2 eggs
medium-grind cornmeal
¼ cup canola oil

Aioli

½ cup mayonnaise
1 teaspoon capers
1 teaspoon sambal paste, or sriracha
fresh-squeezed juice of ½ lemon

Preheat oven to 450°F. Place cod on parchment-lined baking sheet. Coat fish with olive oil and a pinch of salt and pepper. Bake for about 10 minutes, until baked through. Let cool. While cod is baking, boil whole potatoes for about 20 minutes. Drain and cool. Sauté onion, red pepper, and celery in 2 tablespoons olive oil. Add dried chili flakes and pinch of salt and pepper, and cook on medium heat for about 20 minutes. Let cool. When the fish, potatoes, and vegetables all are cooled to room temperature, combine in a large bowl. Add eggs and, using your hands, mix everything well. Chill for 30 minutes. Place cornmeal in a separate large bowl and add a teaspoon of salt and pepper. Using a large soup spoon, scoop the cod-potato mixture and roll in the cornmeal. Form patties with your hands and place on the parchment-lined baking sheet. This should make about a dozen cod cakes. Heat canola oil in a large sauté pan to about 350°F or just until the oil ripples. Sear each cod cake for 2 minutes per side, until golden. Place on the baking sheet. When all are seared, bake for 15 minutes in a 350°F oven. While they are baking, mix together aioli ingredients. Serves 6.

Provincetown Tennessee Williams Theater Festival

Writer Tennessee Williams spent the summers of 1940, '41, '44, and '47 in Provincetown perfecting his craft. He wrote to his agent Audrey Wood in 1944: "I am moving into a little shanty in the dunes where I can avoid the summer crowds. I find this is a good place to work, and think I will get a play off to you next week." During that time, Williams worked prodigiously on short stories, poems, and plays that have become enduring classics, including *A Streetcar Named Desire* and *The Glass Menagerie*. He also began writing *The Night of the Iguana* and *Suddenly Last Summer* there.

The Provincetown Tennessee Williams Theater Festival was founded in 2006 by theater director and Williams scholar David Kaplan, along with a group of theater professionals and community members. The festival's mission, which takes place each September two weeks before Columbus Day, is to advance the spirit of Tennessee Williams through productions of his known and unknown plays, the works of his peers, and modern works he has inspired. "Williams began writing *The Parade* in the summer of 1940 when he was living in Provincetown, and the play is set on the beach," Kaplan says. "Actually performed on Provincetown Beach, it viscerally shares with the audience the inspiration Williams found in Provincetown. The enduring sight of the water and the sky is as much the essence of the playwright's vision as the short-lived joys and sorrows of his summer love story." The world premiere of *The Parade* in 2006 was the highlight of the festival's first season. An audience favorite, this play was also performed at the 2007, 2011, and 2015 festivals.

Tennessee Williams Theater Festival box office on Commercial Street

Nash Hightower (*standing*) as Dick and Ben Berry as Don perform in the 2015 production of *The Parade* on Provincetown Beach. *Photo by Josh Andrus*

A unique aspect of the festival is what producing director Charlene Donaghy calls "found space." In addition to local theaters and the beach, it may include stages built from scratch for performances in homes, gardens, and porches. Star power comes by the likes of award-winning actress Kathleen Turner, a returning guest who gives on-stage acting classes. Performing artists and Tennessee Williams scholars come from as near by as Wellfleet and as far away as Cyprus, Japan, and Cape Town, South Africa. In 2019, audience members came from thirty-three states and six countries.

Each festival is organized around a theme. "Wishful Thinking" explored the drama of anticipation by pairing Williams's plays with pieces by Anton Chekhov and Samuel Beckett. The program "Tennessee Williams and Shakespeare" helped audiences make connections between the two playwrights. "Beyond Success" paired lesser-known, underappreciated works by Williams and Eugene O'Neill. Another festival theme, "Does Fear Have an Aesthetic?," paired works by Williams and Yukio Mishima. The two men visited each other, saw each other's plays, and shared collaborators. In 1957–58, when Williams met Mishima while working on *Suddenly Last Summer*, Williams entered what some call his Japanese phase. This period of Japanese influence ran for a dozen years until 1970, when Mishima died. The well-known plays by Williams from this period, including *Suddenly Last Summer* and *The Night of the Iguana* (1961) echo the Japanese Noh theater's invocation of demons who appear to protagonists in fever dreams. For more information: http://twptown.org.

Mawuli Semevo performs as Mr. Gutman in the Williams play *Camino Real. Photo by Josh Andrus*

The Lobster Pot Restaurant in Provincetown is popular for pre-theater dining. Light or hearty fare is offered to satisfy any appetite. Here is a recipe from owner Tim McNulty's ***Lobster Pot Cookbook***. Courtesy of Tim McNulty, chef/owner of the Lobster Pot Restaurant. Recipes are written as they appear in the book.

Sea Clam Chili

1½ pounds chopped tomatoes, canned
½–¾ pounds dark-red kidney beans, cooked
6 tablespoons tomato paste
¼ cup soybean oil
1 tablespoon garlic, pureed
4 ounces canned green chilies, chopped
1¼ cup onions, small dice
¾ cup celery, small dice
½ cup green bell pepper, small dice
5 tablespoons chili powder
5 tablespoons taco seasonings
1 cup veal stock
2 pounds fresh sea clams, chopped (save juice)
salt and pepper to taste
additional veal or clam stock for desired consistency

In a 4-quart pot, sauté the garlic, onion, celery, green peppers, and chilies in the oil until the onions are translucent. Do not brown. Add the seasonings and stir. Add the beans, tomatoes, and stock, and stir. Cook for 10–15 minutes. Add the clams and juice and cook until just tender. Add salt and pepper and additional stock as needed. Serve with a dollop of sour cream or crème fraiche. Yields 12 cups.

Nantucket Cranberry Festival

When Mother Nature wields her crimson paintbrush over autumn cranberry bogs, it's a sight like no other. The brilliant red of flooded bogs is spectacular as harvesters detach berries from submerged vines and they float to the surface. At the Nantucket Cranberry Festival, visitors are invited not only to tour the bogs, but to grab waders and help with the wet harvest. The Milestone Cranberry Bog, near the center of the island, is transformed into a magical area for this family-friendly event. There are self-guided bog tours with experts on hand at different locations to answer questions and point out interesting facts. Harvesting demonstrations, family activities, hayrides, live music, and antique harvesting-equipment displays add to the attractions. Kids can compete in sack races, tug-of-war, and more. Food purveyors offer all manner of cranberry creations, from backyard BBQ to cranberry-tinged Asian food to bakery sweets. Of course, fresh organic cranberries are available for sale.

Kids enjoy cranberry activities throughout the day. *Photo by Eleanor Hallewell*

Nantucket has a long tradition of growing cranberries. *Photo by Eleanor Hallewell*

NANTUCKET
Locally
GROWN
SINCE
1857
CRANBERRIES
NANTUCKET CONSERVATION FOUNDATION

First cultivated on Cape Cod in 1816 by Captain Henry Hall, a Revolutionary War veteran, cranberries weren't produced commercially on Nantucket until 1857. We read in *Yesterday's Island, Today's Nantucket* (October/November 2019) that by 1914, "Nantucket was home to the world's largest contiguous cranberry bog. Producers were harvesting 8,000–10,000 barrels of cranberries a year from 300 acres. Nantucket was an ideal place for them to grow, owing in part to the naturally wet and boggy valleys of the island's moors." Today, twenty-four separate bogs totaling 195 acres are under the care of the Nantucket Conservation Foundation. The 50-acre Milestone Cranberry Bog is the largest and oldest continually operated farm on the island. The foundation boasts that it is the largest certified organic cranberry grower in the United States. The annual Nantucket Cranberry Festival, on Saturday of Columbus Day weekend, celebrates the island's berry-harvesting past as well as modern-day production. For more information: www.nantucketconservation.org/events/cranberry-festival.

Visitors get a close-up look at the Milestone cranberry bog.

Harvesting berries.
Photo by Eleanor Hallewell

Wicked Island Bakery is an award-winning bakery on Nantucket Island, owned and operated by Ben and Heather Woodbury and their native daughters Emma and Adelaide. Heather's family has lived on the island for generations. Ben, a pastry chef from New York City whose career included working at some of New York's finest restaurants, came to the island to work at the legendary 21 Federal Restaurant. Since striking out on their own with Wicked Island Bakery in 2013, the couple has earned a reputation for fine, scratch-made pastries both sweet and savory, and the affection of their patrons. Their baked goods are popular at the Nantucket Cranberry Festival.

Cranberry Scones and Orange Flower Glaze

Courtesy of Wicked Island Bakery, Nantucket

Cranberry Scones and Orange Flower Glaze

½ cup dried cranberries
½ cup orange juice
2¾ cups high-gluten flour
1 tablespoon baking powder
¼ cup sugar
½ teaspoon salt
½ cup butter
2 eggs
½ cup heavy cream
1 cup 10X confectioner's sugar
2 tablespoons water
1 teaspoon orange flower water

Preheat oven to 375°F. Soak cranberries in orange juice, then set aside. In food processor, process flour, baking powder, sugar, and salt (2–3 pulses.) Add cold cubed butter; process until completely cut in. In large mixing bowl, whisk together eggs and cream. Add dry mix to wet in mixing bowl. Add cranberries. Mix with spatula until dough forms. Don't overmix. Turn out onto lightly floured surface; pat into rectangle. With a knife, cut 3-inch triangles and arrange evenly on a nonstick baking sheet; brush with cream. Bake until golden, 15–18 minutes. Stir together 10X sugar, water, and orange flower water to make a smooth glaze. Glaze scones while still warm.

Yarmouth Seaside Festival

In 1978, longtime Yarmouth resident Jan Butler realized that many Cape Cod towns had festivals, but lamented that her town did not. With the hope of developing community spirit, she put an ad in the local paper, asking for volunteers to help her develop a town festival. The story goes that seventeen people showed up. Butler went before the town selectmen to pitch her idea. Everyone supported her, but one selectman commented, "It will never happen in Yarmouth."

"That's all it took," she says. Now more than forty years old, the festival still has some of the original volunteers onboard. Occurring every Columbus Day weekend, it has grown into a three-day gala, and Butler's dream of a fun-filled weekend for families is as strong as ever. She says, "I know many people love the festival, come back year after year, and bring their kids and grandkids."

The festival kicks off on Saturday with a juried arts-and-crafts fair composed of more than one hundred vendors from all over the US. Children's tents offer puppet, clown, and magic shows. The Raptor Project is just one example of the educational programs on deck. Crowds surround Jonathan

A young visitor helps Jonathon Cook feed his American eagle at his Raptor Project show.

The Cape Cod Highland Light Scottish Pipe Band is a parade hit.

Cook as he shares interesting facts about his extraordinary array of eagles, hawks, falcons, and owls. After a full day of activities, participants can relax on Bass River Beach in the glow of the traditional bonfire. On Sunday, thousands of spectators line traffic-free Route 28 from Captain Parker's Restaurant to the Massachusetts State Police Barracks to enjoy a parade of marching bands, themed floats, antique cars, and performers.

Monday's events include a kayak and canoe race, starting at Bass River Beach in South Yarmouth and finishing at Wilbur Park. Rain or shine, the order of the day is that boaters must have fun. And they do! Landlubbers are invited to gather shovels, pails, rakes, and imagination for the sand sculpture contest on the beach. When asked why he volunteers with the festival, Craig Jasie, says, "I love the old Cape Cod feel. At no cost or hassle, parents and kids can have a great time while building memories." For more information: https://yarmouthseasidefestival.com.

An artist puts finishing touches on her sand sculpture. *Photo courtesy of Jan Butler*

Rain or shine, the kayak race is always fun. *Photo courtesy of Jan Butler*

Captain Parker's is one of Cape Cod's favorite eating establishments. After watching the festival parade in front of the restaurant on Route 28, many people head there to have lunch. Here is a recipe inspired by one of Captain Parker's popular dishes.

Cape Cod Reuben

12 ounces bottle lager beer
1⅓ cups flour, separated
½ teaspoon salt
1 teaspoon paprika
3 cups coleslaw mix
½ cup coleslaw dressing
4 cups vegetable oil for frying
4 6-ounce cod fish fillets
8 slices marble rye bread
4 slices Swiss cheese

In a large bowl, whisk the beer, 1 cup flour, salt, and paprika until smooth. Chill for 30 minutes. In another bowl combine the slaw mix and dressing. Preheat the broiler for toasting bread. Meanwhile, in a deep skillet, heat the oil to 375°F. Place the remaining ⅓ cup flour on a large plate. Working one at a time, coat the fish with flour, shaking off excess, then coat with the beer batter. Lower the fish carefully into the hot oil and cook until brown and crispy, turning once for a total of approximately 5 minutes. Place bread on the baking sheet; broil until toasted. Transfer toasted side down onto work surface. Top with fish, cheese, and coleslaw. Add another toasted slice of bread on top, toasted side up. Serves 4.

Cape Cod Reuben

Wellfleet OysterFest

In 1606, Samuel de Champlain explored the Outer Cape town of Wellfleet and named it Port Aux Huitres (Oyster Port) for its bountiful oyster population. Three hundred years later, Guglielmo Marconi built America's first transatlantic radio transmitter station on the high bluffs overlooking the great outer beach. In 1961, President Kennedy created Cape Cod National Seashore that spans the length of the town. Another Wellfleet legacy is its famously tasty oysters. Fine restaurants from New York to Paris agree that Wellfleet oysters (*Crassostrea virginica*) are some of the world's best. What makes them more special than similar species from Long Island, the Chesapeake Bay, or even Canada's Maritime provinces? Cold, clean water; high salinity; big, fast-moving tides, and the rich variety of phytoplankton on which they feed.

The weekend after Columbus Day, all Cape Cod roads lead to the Wellfleet OysterFest to celebrate the usually sedate town's oyster and shellfishing traditions. The event is organized by Wellfleet SPAT (Shellfish Promotion and Tasting), a nonprofit chartered in 2002 to sustain Wellfleet's shellfishing and aquaculture industries. This popular fall event offers something for everyone. Shell fishermen and women come in off the flats to offer their briny catch of oysters and clams. Pop-up raw bars and restaurants serve oysters, chowders, and stuffed clams. Chefs offer cooking demonstrations.

The food and fun at Oysterfest attracts thousands of visitors.

You can buy from one to a dozen fresh oysters from the many local shell fisherman at the Wellfleet Oysterfest.

Sheila's Oyster Farm
Wellfleet, Ma
Sheila's Oyster Farm
Wellfleet, Ma

Andrew Cummings's Wash-Ashore Oyster Ranch in Wellfleet. *Photo by Julia Cumes*

A major goal of Oysterfest is to educate the public about marine life and fisheries.

Of course, the classic accompaniment to oysters is beer and ale, and there is plenty on hand from New England producers. Juried artisans show and sell a range of crafts, including jewelry, pottery, clothing, and paintings. On the more serious side, top experts in marine science present talks on environmental issues. Perhaps the most popular attraction is the Oyster Shuck Off on Saturday and Sunday. Amateurs compete for the fun of it, but serious hometown shuckers are known to go on to compete nationally. Proceeds from the event support SPAT's educational mission, which includes college scholarships and community grants. For more information: https://wellfleetspat.org/wellfleet-oysterfest-homepage.

The Wicked Oyster restaurant on Main Street was established in 2004. The structure housing the main dining room dates back to 1750 and was floated across the bay from Billingsgate Island, now visible only as a sandbar at low tide. While adding their own touches to the building, the owners have been careful to honor its rich history and provide the ambiance of a Cape Cod home. One can find the Wicked Oyster under the food tent during Wellfleet OysterFest, usually serving up their buttermilk fried oysters and clam chowder. Recipe courtesy of the Wicked Oyster.

Oyster Stew

2 tablespoons olive oil
1 cup carrots, diced
1 cup celery, diced
1 cup leeks, diced
1 cup frozen peas
1 cup frozen corn
1 star anise pod
24 Wellfleet oysters shucked, and brine reserved
6 cups heavy cream
2 tablespoons olive oil

Wellfleet oysters are prized the world over.

Pour oil into a large saucepan and sauté carrots, celery, leeks, peas, corn, and star anise on medium-low heat until soft (5–7 minutes.) Do not brown. Turn heat to high and add cream. Bring to slow boil and reduce cream, 3–4 minutes, being careful not to let it boil over. After cream has thickened slightly, add oysters and brine. Bring just to boiling point and remove from heat. Remove star anise pod. Serve immediately with crusty bread. Serves 4–6.

Martha's Vineyard Food and Wine Festival

On a chilly afternoon in late October, the streets of downtown Edgartown are usually deserted. But during the Martha's Vineyard Food and Wine Festival, the scene is very different. At the signature Grand Tasting Event, held at the Winnetu Ocean Resort, one of several festival venues in the town, more than 2,000 food-and-wine enthusiasts fill three sprawling tents. Culinary experts and more than 250 vintners and wine merchants arrive from around the world, and participants enjoy endless finger foods and bottomless vintages. Tastings range from brown-buttered lobster over grits, to Wagyu beef tartar with lemon sabayon, to sugar-coated doughnuts and champagne. In spite of the sellout crowd, it's intimate enough for visitors to talk with the chefs and vintners.

Amy Traverso, *Yankee Magazine* senior food editor, speaks to diners at Lobsterpalooza. *Photo by Joshua Robinson-White*

Each year the festival's wine portfolio includes high-quality wines from all over the world.

Chef Brendan Vesey of Joinery and Botanica restaurants in Portsmouth, New Hampshire, puts finishing touches on his Wagyu beef tartare with lemon sabayon and juniper cracker.

Finger foods at the Grand Tasting come in all shapes and sizes.

Five days are filled with classes, cooking demonstrations, dinners, and more. A recent festival featured a Chefs Know Fish Dinner pairing wine and seafood, with a discussion about sustainability. International themes included A Taste of Japan, celebrating the country's varied cuisine in five courses, and Europe Meets South America with Biodynamic Wines. Ticket prices are not cheap: a dinner might run $250, the Grand Tasting $150, but tickets start selling in May and most events sell out. Celebrity culinary experts offering seminars and demonstrations are a popular draw. Sam Sifton, food editor for the *New York Times* and founding editor of NYT Cooking, was a recent speaker. Amy Traverso, *Yankee Magazine* senior food editor, hosted Lobsterpalooza, where attendees sampled three styles of lobster roll. While some chefs come from off-island, it's certain the seafood and vegetables are island-grown.

The organized walks and tours between courses are a good way to work off all those calories. The Food and Wine Festival is a festival with a mission. The festival honors the island's rich lineage of farming and fishing, and a portion of the proceeds benefit Island Grown Schools, which offers hands-on farm experience to almost every school-aged child in the community. Another beneficiary is the Martha's Vineyard Agricultural Society's Farmer's Program, which provides vital funding and resources to island farmers. For more information: https://mvfoodandwine.com.

Wild-Boar Meatballs with Cilantro Sauce

Courtesy of Chef Brian Poe / Tip Tap Room

Acclaimed chef Brian Poe is the chef/owner of the Tip Tap Room in Boston's Beacon Hill neighborhood. These delicious wild-boar meatballs were popular at a recent Martha's Vineyard Food and Wine Festival Grand Tasting Event. Chef Poe says home cooks can easily substitute pork for the main ingredient. This recipe is party size but can be cut in half.

Wild Board Meatballs with Cilantro Sauce

Meatballs

¼ cup chipotle peppers
1 small bunch cilantro
6 ounces lime juice
5 pounds Fossil Farms wild-boar ground meat
8 ounces panko bread crumbs
salt and pepper to taste

Puree chipotle peppers, cilantro, and lime juice in food processer and combine with wild boar. Add bread crumbs and mix until blended. Portion into 2-ounce balls and roast at 350°F for 15 minutes. Set aside.

Meatball Sauce

1 cup chili ginger sauce (recipe follows)
1 cup pickled serrano chiles (recipe follows)
1 cup water
1 cup veal stock
1 bunch cilantro

Pickled Serrano Chilies

1 cup rice wine vinegar
6 serrano chili peppers, chopped
1 bay leaf
Pinch each of pink peppercorn, black peppercorn, and coriander

Using a medium-sized pot, bring vinegar to boil. Add chopped serrano pepper and seasonings. Remove from heat and let cool.

Chili Ginger Sauce

2 ounces garlic, minced
2 ounces ginger, minced
1 cup vegetable stock
1 cup rice wine vinegar
1 cup sugar
¼ cup fish sauce
2 ounces tomato paste
4 ounces green-label Asian sauce (chili garlic paste)

Sauté garlic and ginger in hot garlic oil. Add all other ingredients, bring to boil, and remove from heat. Puree the mixture and cool. Combine chili ginger sauce, pickled serrano chiles, water, and veal stock and simmer for 1 hour. Cool and add chopped cilantro.

Serrano Salsa

2 Roma tomatoes, diced
½ bunch cilantro
6 pickled serrano chiles
1 lime, juiced
Pinch of salt and pepper

Combine all ingredients and reserve.

To serve, add the meatballs to the sauce and heat. Serve with serrano salsa.

Eastham Turnip Festival

The Cape Cod town of Eastham is known as the place where Mayflower Pilgrims and Native Americans had their first skirmish in 1620. But not many people know about their prize crop, the Eastham turnip. First, you have to forget those bitter-tasting, overcooked cubes offered at the Thanksgiving table. The Eastham turnip, with its creamy white body and magenta-tinged crown, is unquestionably king of the homegrown crops, regaled as being the sweetest, mildest, and tastiest in the universe. Local lore has it that the porous, sweet, sandy soil in North Eastham works its magic on the root vegetable, producing its delectable taste. Each November on the Saturday before Thanksgiving, Eastham Friends of the Public Library and dozens of cooks, organizers, and volunteers put on a festival to celebrate this prize crop. And what a down-home shindig it is!

Opposite: Mr. and Mrs. Turnip are always happy to pose for photographs.

Crafts

This event, intentionally quirky, usually begins with a tongue-in-cheek Blessing of the Turnips and a crowning of the year's Turnip King and Queen. Bluegrass music fills the massive Nauset Regional High School gymnasium, and Mr. and Mrs. Turnip happily pose for selfies with guests. Dozens of vendors and local farmers have tables with mountainous piles of fall produce and baked goods. Juried artisans offer all manner of art and craft items. Turnip-themed contests include the Turnip Shuck-Off (speed of peeling) and the Enormous Turnip Weight Guessing challenge. Middle-school and high-school students play a large role each year in helping younger fairgoers with games such as turnip bowling, connect four turnips, and turnip hole. A highlight is the Turnip Cook-Off, where local restaurants vie for prizes by inventing tantalizing dishes that appeal to even the most-hesitant turnip eaters. Entries have incorporated turnips into crepes, stews, slaws, casseroles, curries, and even cheesecake. "We've seen it all," says event chair Marianne Sinopoli. Naturally, Eastham turnips are for sale, and lines are usually very long. For more information: https://easthamturnipfestival.com.

Bob Wells and his giant turnip.
Photo courtesy of Eastham Public Library

EASTHAM TURNIP HISTORY

Eastham turnip farming has a long history. The 1905 crop of 10,710 bushels ranked Eastham first in Barnstable County. Along with asparagus, turnip farming was what most Eastham men did. Turnips were planted in early July after the asparagus was harvested. To generate seeds for the next year, farmers would put the best turnips (untrimmed) into pits dug below the freeze line, and cover them with seaweed and sand. In spring, the turnips were dug up and replanted in the fields, where they produced shoots, flowers, and seed-filled pods.

Lines are long to purchase fresh Eastham turnips.

Portioning samples of Harvest Turnip Slaw

Besides being loaded with nutrients, turnips are delicious if cooked the right way. These prize-winning recipes from the Eastham Turnip Festival elevate these root vegetables from the bottom of the vegetable bin to a place of honor on the dinner table. Recipes courtesy of Marianne Sinopoli, festival director and Eastham Library outreach coordinator.

Eastham Turnip Puff Casserole

Grand prize, Mac's Parties & Provisions

6 cups peeled Eastham turnip cubes
4 tablespoons butter, divided
2 eggs, beaten
3 tablespoons flour
1 tablespoon brown sugar
1 teaspoon baking powder
salt and pepper
pinch of fresh ground nutmeg
½ cup panko

Cook turnips until soft. Drain well, mash, and add 2 tablespoons butter. When turnips have cooled, add the beaten eggs, flour, sugar, baking powder, spices, and salt and pepper. Put mixture in buttered baking dish. Melt remaining 2 tablespoons butter in pan, add panko, and cook slowly until panko browns.

Season with salt and pepper. Spread on top of turnip mixture. Bake at 375°F for about 30 minutes until crumbs are browned. Serves 4–6.

Curried Turnip Bisque

People's Choice Award, Rock Harbor Grill

1 stick unsalted butter, cubed
1 large yellow onion, sliced thin
1 quart water
3 pounds Eastham turnips, peeled and diced
1 pound carrots, peeled and diced
½ cup honey
2 cups heavy cream
1 tablespoon ground dry ginger
1½ teaspoons ground cardamom
1½ teaspoons ground cloves
1½ teaspoons ground turmeric
2 tablespoons curry powder, toasted
kosher salt, to taste

Melt butter in a saucepan over medium heat. Add onions and cook until translucent but not brown. Add water, turnips, and carrots and turn heat to high. Bring to a boil and reduce to a simmer. Cook until carrots and turnips are very soft. Add honey, spices, and heavy cream. Simmer 10–15 minutes and remove from heat. Blend with an immersion blender until smooth. Adjust seasoning to taste with salt, honey, or spices.

Christmas on Cape Cod and the Islands

The Provincetown Lobster Pot Tree lights up Lopes Square. *Photo courtesy of Crystal Popko*

The warm season that brings most visitors to Cape Cod may be over, but for those who visit or remain for the holidays, it's a time of enchantment. The region's rich maritime lineage plays a role in most festivities and even how Santa arrives. Here are some highlights.

Cape Cod

The lighting of the 252-foot Provincetown Monument, typically on the day before Thanksgiving, celebrates the arrival of the Pilgrims in 1620. More than 3,000 lights are strung on nineteen strands from top to bottom; they shine every night through January 6, representing the five weeks the Pilgrims spent in Provincetown before setting sail for Plymouth.

A short distance away on Lopes Square, the Lobster Pot Tree adds to the holiday glow of this Outer Cape town. Started in 2003 by Julian Popko as a tribute to Provincetown's hard-working lobstermen, the two-story tree is decorated with 3,400 LED lights and 135 lobster traps on loan from local lobstermen.

At the other end of the Cape, Holly Days in Sandwich is a monthlong celebration with caroling, a cookie stroll, and the lighting of the Littlest Christmas Tree in the middle of Shawme Pond. Michael Magyar's towering outdoor lighted wire sculptures, or Giants, as they are known, welcome winter travelers all along Route 6A. Heritage Museums and Gardens in Sandwich helps families create their own traditions by offering a spin on the vintage carousel or a photo op with Santa in a Model T Ford. The museum's Gardens Aglow offers beautiful holiday light displays on the 100-acre grounds.

How else would Santa arrive on this nautical realm than by sea? Vessels adorned with sparkling lights take part in Santa's Boat Parade as he arrives in Hyannis Harbor in early December. Other Santa arrivals take place in Falmouth Harbor and the Chatham Fish Pier. At A Seaside Christmas in Orleans, one can even enjoy a pancake breakfast with Mrs. Claus while waiting for Santa to arrive at Town Cove. The Bass River in South Yarmouth is the backdrop for the Annual Holiday Cookie Stroll. Visitors can explore the town and enjoy fresh-baked cookies and fill a take-home bag at participating stops. The South

One of Michael Magyar's "giants."
Photo courtesy of Michael Magyar

Santa arrives at the Chatham Fish Pier.

Yarmouth Library offers a nice rest with a cup of hot cider. The Cultural Center of Cape Cod is filled with artistic creations and crafts for last-minute shoppers.

Not slowing down after Christmas, Cape Cod welcomes the New Year with First Night celebrations from Sandwich to Provincetown. Sandwich hosts multicultural activities in venues all around town. The Reveler's Parade travels down Main Street to the historic Town Hall. Chatham offerings include a town photo at the Chatham Lighthouse and a day of entertainment and fireworks at the stroke of midnight at Oyster Pond. Provincetown's extravaganza includes ice skating, dance parties, and the Polar Bear Plunge. For more information: www.capecodchamber.org/events/featured-events/christmas-on-cape-cod.

Martha's Vineyard

At the annual Oak Bluffs Tree Lighting in Post Office Square, hundreds of kids and parents, festooned in red antlers, enjoy hot chocolate and sing Christmas carols. A blaring siren announces Santa's arrival via fire truck. Oak Bluff landscaper Mark Crossland and his team created a winter wonderland by erecting dozens of "light trees" in Ocean Park, with lights synchronized to music.

Christmas on Martha's Vineyard. *Photo by Michael Blanchard*

More than a hundred island businesses participate in the annual Christmas in Edgartown weekend festival. A forty-year-old tradition, the event raises more than $50,000 for charities and nonprofits. Holiday shopping specials, horse and wagon rides, wreath making, cookie decorating, lighthouse and Japanese garden tours, photos with the iconic Black Dog (and Santa, of course) are all on the bill. For more information: http://edgartownboardoftrade.com/events/christmas-in-edgartown.

Nantucket

Nantucket is at its most beautiful during the holidays. The Christmas Stroll, held the first full weekend in December, kicks off the festive season. Begun more than four decades ago to keep residents from leaving the island to buy gifts, shopkeepers kept stores open late the first Friday in December. People could shop while enjoying a cup of mulled cider, wine, or holiday sweets. The event now lasts through the weekend, attracting some 10,000 visitors. Starting the day after Thanksgiving, more than one hundred 7-foot trees are erected along downtown streets, leading to a giant tree on Main Street decorated by a local artist. Endowed with "magical powers," it even talks to passersby.

On Saturday, when Main Street is closed to traffic, costumed carolers create a Currier and Ives vibe. Santa arrives by boat and rides to the Jared Coffin House to hear what's on children's wish lists while they enjoy hot chocolate and candy canes.

The Whaling Museum is transformed into a winter wonderland for the entire month of December. The twenty-five-year-old Festival of Trees features approximately one hundred Christmas trees whimsically designed by area artists and merchants. The museum also showcases local talent in its Festival of Wreaths. Visitors bid in a silent auction for their favorites. Proceeds benefit the Nantucket Historical Association. For more information: www.nantucketchamber.org/stroll.

The name of this cookie, from Nantucket chef Ben Woodbury, is a play on words. Tuckernuck is an island and former whaling port off Nantucket. Its name allegedly means "a loaf of bread." This is a colorful and delicious addition to any holiday cookie collection.

TUCKERnut Cookies

Courtesy of Ben Woodbury, chef/owner,
Wicked Island Bakery

TUCKERnut cookies

1 cup butter
1 cup brown sugar
½ cup granulated sugar
2 eggs
1 teaspoon vanilla
2½ cups flour
½ teaspoon baking soda
¼ teaspoon salt
1½ cups chocolate chips
1½ cups pecans
1 cup cranberries, roughly chopped

Preheat oven to 325°F. In a large bowl, cream together the butter and sugars until fluffy. Slowly add the eggs and vanilla. In a separate bowl, mix the dry ingredients. Add them to the egg mixture and blend, scraping sides and bottom of bowl. Add chocolate chips, pecans, and cranberries, using a spatula or mixer on low speed. Scoop 2–3-ounce dough balls onto nonstick cookie sheet. Bake for 10–12 minutes.

Other Festivals of Note

Photo courtesy of Carol Williams, Chocolate Fest

Osterville Chocolate Fest

What could be a better antidote to winter blues than a piece of kir-soaked chocolate raspberry cake, or chocolate cheesecake filled with chocolate ganache. These are just two of the delicacies that might be served at the Osterville Chocolate Fest, held the Saturday before Valentine's Day. While many shops in the village offer chocolate tastings, the main event is the chocolate dessert contest, usually held in the Osterville Library. Adults and children compete to win gift cards and other prizes. The event is one of many that the Osterville Business and Professional Association sponsors during the year. For more information: www.ostervillevillage.com.

Brewster in Bloom

In the mid-1980s, a group of Brewster business owners marked the beginning of spring by planting hundreds of daffodils along Route 6A, and Brewster in Bloom was born. Now in its thirty-fifth year, the three-day festival on the first weekend in May raises money for the community. Past festivals have funded the construction of the bandstand at Drummer Boy Park and local scholarships. The Brewster Band kicks things off with a rousing concert. Businesses, museums, and organizations offer demonstrations and exhibits. Runners and walkers participate in Saturday morning's 5K Bloom Run. The Art and Antique trail is an opportunity to chat with artists and experts at the town's many antique and art galleries. More than ninety arts-and-crafts vendors set up tents to exhibit their work. In addition to the kid-fest at Drummer Boy Park, Sunday's Main Street parade is a highlight, with prizes for "Best in Show," "Most Creative," and "Best Interpretation of Theme." For more information: https://brewster-capecod.com/brewster-events/brewster-in-bloom/

5K Bloom Run. *Photo by William Pomeroy*

ArtWeek Cape Cod

ArtWeek Massachusetts, a statewide celebration in late April and early May, includes a hundred Cape Cod–based events in more than twenty communities from Bourne to Provincetown. Attendees enjoy arts and culture with hands-on, interactive performances. A small sample of happenings might include the following:

Upper Cape: Plein air painting, needle art workshops, glass-blowing, publishing workshops, outdoor music strolls

Mid Cape: Symphony open rehearsal, writer's workshops, sea captain walking tours, colored sand art

Lower Cape: Historic house sketch session, digital-photo workshop, bird carving, rug braiding, artist marketing sessions

Outer Cape: Staged theater readings, lantern making, tapestry weaving, vocal lessons, lighthouse photo sessions

For more information: www.artweekma.org.

Rhododendron Festival

Heritage Museums and Gardens in Sandwich is host to this annual late-May-to-early-June festival celebrating one of the largest collections of rhododendrons in the US. Thousands of blooms in more than one hundred varieties cover the museum's 100 acres of woodland and pond trails. Walking tours, pruning demonstrations, and landscape ideas are offered, and rare Charles Dexter and Jack Cowles rhododendron hybrids are for sale. Programs are free with museum admission. For more information: https://heritagemuseumsandgardens.org/event/rhododendron-festival-2.

Community Drum Circle for Healing. *Photo courtesy of Sue Sullivan, ARTWEEK*

Rhododendrons in full bloom

Cape Cod Quahog Day

Each first day of summer since 2009, Doug the Quahog emerges at a Cape Cod location with his security detail, a team of black-suited men and women with clamming rakes. During this tongue-in-cheek "prognostication ceremony," his human sidekick, Captain Johnny Quahog of the Quahog Republic, lifts the little soothsayer to his ear to hear him whisper how many days of beach weather are ahead. Sponsored by the Cape Cod Chamber of Commerce, this event is fun for the whole family. Locations of the event vary from year to year. For more information: www.capecodchamber.org/cape-cod-quahog-day.

Nantucket Film Festival

Founded in 1996 by Nantucket siblings Jill and Jonathan Burkhart, the popular Nantucket Film Festival (NFF) in late June honors the art of screenwriting and storytelling with original and live events. Producers, screenwriters, actors, agents, and fans gather on this "faraway island" to enjoy films ranging from dramas to comedies to thought-provoking documentaries. In addition to films, festival offerings include panels, parties, storytelling events, and awards. A recent Comedy Roundtable featured *Saturday Night Live* writers and performers and took participants behind the scenes, sharing some of the best *SNL* sketches that didn't or couldn't air. Previous favorite films that premiered at the NFF include *Whale Rider*, *The Full Monty*, *Boyhood*, and *Next Stop Wonderland*. For more information: http://nantucketfilmfestival.org.

Nantucket Film Festival poster

Above: Doug the Quahog predicts the summer. *Photo courtesy of William DeSousa-Mauk on behalf of Cape Cod Chamber of Commerce*

Cape Cod Canal Day by the Railroad Bridge

Cape Cod Canal Day in mid-September invites everyone to celebrate this world-famous waterway and its environs. Several thousand people descended on Buzzards Bay Park to participate in the inaugural event in 2018, and it's been growing since. The family-friendly park is adjacent to the unique Cape Cod Railroad Bridge, an art deco vertical-lift bridge built in 1933. Organized by the Canal Region Chamber of Commerce, this one-day event features live entertainment, including several of the nearby Massachusetts Maritime Academy's music bands, a cornhole tournament, and arts-and-crafts vendors. The beautiful kids' playground provides hours of fun for youngsters. Local food trucks, craft beer, and wine purveyors are on hand to satisfy hungry visitors. For more information: www.capecodcanalchamber.org.

Canal Day visitors at Buzzards Bay Park

Listening to music on the Community Center fields, Harwich

Harwich Cranberry Art and Music Festival

Formerly called the Harwich Cranberry Festival, this two-day event in mid-September includes plenty of art and music to merit the name change. Funk, rock, bluegrass—it's all here for music lovers to listen or dance to. The new location for the aptly named Cranjam behind the Harwich Community Center provides plenty of seating on the grass and under the tent. Along with music, there are over 150 vendors selling handcrafted items. For hungry festivalgoers, the dining court hosts all variety of food trucks. The beer and wine garden, featuring locally crafted beer, is stocked to meet the needs of the 10,000 visitors reported to attend each year. The event's popularity has gone far beyond Cape Cod and the Islands. In

1986, at the festival's tenth anniversary, the mayor of Harwich, England, Harwich's sister town, came here to enjoy the experience. For more information: www.harwichcranberryartsandmusicfestival.org/schedule.

Provincetown Book Festival

This festival offers three full days of events for readers, writers, and book lovers of all kinds. According to Nan Cinnater, lead librarian at the Provincetown Public Library, which sponsors the event, "The festival celebrates books and those who write them. We feel we're carrying on in the tradition of the Provincetown Players and Charles Hawthorne's Cape School of Art by making room for new voices to be heard, and real questions about life and art discussed." She adds, "We also have an opportunity to bring to Provincetown a diverse group of authors writing about and discussing contemporary issues. Combining different voices is what makes the festival so special."

The event usually opens on Friday evening with a reading and reception for the recipient of the Rose Dorothea Award, given annually by the Board of Library Trustees to an outstanding author from or influenced by the Outer Cape. On Saturday and Sunday there are scheduled readings and conversations with award-winning regional authors and other guests. Throughout both Saturday and Sunday, book aficionados can enjoy the giant book sale on the library lawn. The event takes place the second weekend in September. For more information: https://provincetownbook festival.org.

PorchFest performers Julie & Denya

Sandwich PorchFest

In keeping with the spirit of the National PorchFest movement, which is to bring communities together through music, the Sandwich PorchFest features guitars, mandolins, drums, bagpipes, concertinas, voices, and more at a dozen porches and storefronts in a walkable area. "I think music is the most nostalgic of the senses. It's a wonderful way to bring people out under pleasant conditions and to celebrate our town," says Joanne Westerhouse, founder of the Sandwich Arts Alliance, which sponsors PorchFest. The event is held on the Sunday of Columbus Day weekend, For more information: www.sandwichartsalliance.org.

NantucketGrown Food Festival

The brainchild of the nonprofit group Sustainable Nantucket, NantucketGrown celebrates the foods and diverse cultures of Nantucket, with the goal of cultivating a sustainable and self-reliant island food system. Over three days in mid-October, local growers and chefs team up to take participants on culinary journeys. At a recent festival, more than fifteen countries were represented in the locally grown foods. Visitors can meet chefs, farmers, bakers, beekeepers, and local food purveyors and participate in farm-to-table dinners, workshops on topics such as fermenting, "root to stem" demonstrations teaching how to use 100 percent of a plant, and an oyster farm boat tour. Also on offer are cocktail classes and tastings of barrel-aged spirits. For more information: www.sustainablenantucket.org.

Farm-to-table display. *Photo courtesy of Tom Richard, Sustainable Nantucket*

Chatham Oktoberfest

Scary and sweet might describe the "pumpkin people" that show up in Kate Gould Park near the bandstand each October, on the second Saturday after Columbus Day and right before Halloween. Fashioned by local businesses, organizations, and other creatives, the festive pumpkins are just a small part of Chatham's Oktoberfest. Old-fashioned crafts and games for kids, the Chatham Town Band, professional entertainers, tasty German fare, food trucks, and, of course, beer add to this celebration of the season. For more information: jennifer@mainsailevents.com.

Halloween in Provincetown

Outlandish garb is pretty much an everyday sighting in Provincetown, but the week before Halloween brings an over-the-top celebration. On Halloween night, Commercial Street comes alive with revelers decked out in fantastic costumes. Pint-sized princesses and pirates in the Greet 'n' Treat parade walk to Motta Field, where decorated vehicles from Provincetown businesses and organizations pass out candy. The haunted bike tour takes participants (on their own bikes) on a 3-mile journey through the town's preternatural night, with tales of ghastly phantoms, haunted homes, and otherworldly encounters. Halloween weekend also features the adult-themed last Tea Dance of the year at the Provincetown boat slip, as well as the Black and Gold Ball in the historic Town Hall. Spooky Bear Weekend celebrates the human variety of *Ursus maritimus* with parties and events before they go into hibernation. For more information: https://ptownevents.com/halloween-provincetown.

Mashpee Oktoberfest

This family-friendly event on the first Saturday in October offers fun fall activities for everyone. Presented by the Mashpee Recreation Department, it takes place on the Mashpee Commons Village Green (across the street from the Mashpee library). From 11 a.m. to 4 p.m., participants enjoy a touch of Deutschland, with a biergarten for adults and foods such as bratwurst and pork shank. Live German music, dancing, and entertainment add to the festive atmosphere. Kids can enjoy train rides, games, puppet shows, and pumpkin decorating. Crafters set up shop in dozens of tents surrounding the lawn. The event is free, and parking is available. For more information: http://mashpeecommons.com/event/mashpee-recreations-2019-oktoberfest.

Sesame Street visits Chatham Oktoberfest

About the Author

Kathryn and her family have been enjoying Cape Cod for 50 years. A full-time resident for over 25 years, she is the author of *Cape Cod and the Islands: Where Beauty and History Meet* (Schiffer Publishing). An artist as well as author, her artwork is in private collections across the United States and abroad. Kathryn and her husband, Charles, live in the town of Sandwich and have three adult children, four grandsons, and a granddaughter.